From The Heart

Christian Song Lyrics

Sherry Norton

WESTBOW
PRESS®
A DIVISION OF THOMAS NELSON
& ZONDERVAN

WestBow Press books may be ordered through booksellers or by contacting:

WestBow Press
A Division of Thomas Nelson & Zondervan
1663 Liberty Drive
Bloomington, IN 47403
www.westbowpress.com
1 (866) 928-1240

ISBN: 978-1-5127-5439-1 (sc)
ISBN: 978-1-5127-5440-7 (hc)
ISBN: 978-1-5127-5438-4 (e)

Library of Congress Control Number: 2016913905

Print information available on the last page.

WestBow Press rev. date: 8/24/2016

Table of Contents

Author's Page

Sheryl (Sherry) Norton was born in October of 1957, the first of three children. At the time of her birth, her parents, were living in Topeka, Kansas assigned to Forbes Air Force Base. She grew up in various places, finally landing in Fayetteville, North Carolina where she now lives. "I really count myself as very Blessed after all I have been through." She is a three times survivor of a form of cancer. She is a widow after 33 years of marriage. She has been visually impaired all her life, "for a long time I was blind not only physically, but spiritually." After being a member of a cult for 23 years, Sherry says only the Love and intervention of Her Heavenly Father brought her out of deception and darkness and trying to live under the law with little love or hope although there was much fear and mans control. The sight I have now in my God I would not trade, though there are times when I wish I could physically see, I have to admit there are other times I am glad that I do not.

Acknowledgements

Above all I acknowledge God Almighty, Lord Jesus Christ and The Holy Spirit. I also believe that the creativity of my earthly parents was handed down to me as well. I must also acknowledge that God's Holy Word has played quite a lot in what has been done here.

Section One

Song Lyrics That Declare And Decree

01. My God is

Verse:
My God is, worthy of all our praise,
My God is holy, and perfect in all His ways.
My God is, the Light brighter
than the sun's rays,
My God is The Ancient of Days.
This is my God, in whom I adore.
He is my God and so much, much more.

Chorus:
My God so true, my God is divine.
My God so pure, my God
is supremely sublime.
Full of grace, mercy, and love so kind.

Verse:
My God, made the universe you see,
My God, hung the sun, moon,
and all the stars to be,
My God, owns gold, silver, and
cattle of a thousand hills freely,
My God, created you and me.
This is my God, of whom I adore.
He is my God, and so much, much more.

Chorus:
My God so true, my God is divine.
My God so pure, my God
is supremely sublime.
Full of grace, mercy, and love so kind.

Verse:
My God, is holding us in His hand,
My God, is wonderfully
made and not by man,
My God, is awesome in the
extreme, clap your hands,
My God, is worthy of praise
shout it o'er the land.
This is my God, of whom I adore.
He is my God, and so much, much more.

Chorus:
My God so true, my God is divine.
My God so pure, my God
is supremely sublime.
Full of grace, mercy, and love so kind.

Bridge:
I Thank you God, for being my God.
I thank you for Your only begotten son.
I thank you Jesus, for taking my place,
so as Your child my God, I can
come seeking Your face.

Chorus:
My God so true, my God is divine.
My God so pure, my God
is supremely sublime.
Full of grace, mercy, and love so kind.

02. *God's Invitation*

Verse:
Launch out into the deep,
cast over thy nets into the water,
you who are God's fishers of men;
expect the best, from our God so bountiful,
our source, our strength, our life.

Verse:
Open your eyes and look
to the fields full of plenty of white,
that is ready for the harvest;
God's calling His human hands and feet,
to the way to Jesus.

Chorus:
The tables are set, and the feast is prepared,
Almighty God has sent out His invitations;
the bride and the Bridegroom bids us come,
and joyfully partake in the Wedding Feast.

First Bridge:
I stand waiting, for you to
receive, the gift of My Son,
choose life and believe.

Chorus:
The tables are set, and the feast is prepared,
Almighty God has sent out His invitations;
the bride and the Bridegroom bids us come,
and joyfully partake in the Wedding Feast.

Verse:
Though sin keeps us from God,
as we accept Jesus Christ as our Lord,
and all that He has done for us,
Jesus' death on the cross
brings us back to Him.
along with His resurrection.

Chorus:
The tables are set, and the feast is prepared,
Almighty God has sent out His invitations;
the bride and the Bridegroom bids us come,
and joyfully partake in the Wedding Feast.

Second Bridge:
Come as you are, seeking My face,
accept My Son,
taking your place.

Chorus:
The tables are set, and the feast is prepared,
Almighty God has sent out His invitations;
the bride and the Bridegroom bids us come,
and joyfully partake in the Wedding Feast.

03. An Awesome Love

Verse:
God loves us even more than life,
proving His love,
through His only begotten Son,
when He came to live,
die, and bear our sins upon Himself,

Verse:
God loves us even more than life,
making Jesus,
the way to come back to Himself,
accept His gift and,
have eternal life with in Our God.

Chorus:
What an awesome love,
what an awesome plan,
for God to redeem man.

Verse:
God loves us even more than life,
when Jesus, died
in our place so that we will live,
seated in heaven
with Jesus, on the right hand of God.

Chorus:
What an awesome love,
what an awesome plan,
for God to redeem man.

Bridge:
Father God is love,
love so pure and true,
He loves us even more than life,
life of His only begotten Son,
accept His gift of love,
and have eternal life in Him also.

Chorus:
What an awesome love,
what an awesome plan,
for God to redeem man.

Chorus:
What an awesome love,
what an awesome plan,
for God to redeem man.

04. Every Step

Chorus:
Each and every step we take,
Brings us ever nearer to Thee.
Each and every choice chosen straight,
Brings us ever nearer to Thee.

Verse:
Closer ever closer
through trial and trouble,
Closer ever closer
through each battle faced.

Chorus:
Each and every step we take,
Brings us ever nearer to Thee.
Each and every choice chosen straight,
Brings us ever nearer to Thee.

Verse:
Closer ever closer
through Your life giving Word,
Closer ever closer
through Your blessed grace.

Chorus:
Each and every step we take,
Brings us ever nearer to Thee.
Each and every choice chosen straight,
Brings us ever nearer to Thee.

Bridge:
Step by Step, and choice by choice,
we walk upon this narrow path,
where Jesus leads, and we follow,
every step closer to You.

Chorus:
Each and every step we take,
Brings us ever nearer to Thee.
Each and every choice chosen straight,
Brings us ever nearer to Thee.

Verse:
Closer ever closer
through Jesus Christ, God's Son,
Closer ever closer
through God's only Son.

Chorus:
Each and every step we take,
Brings us ever nearer to Thee.
Each and every choice chosen straight,
Brings us ever nearer to Thee.

05. In Jesus's Name

Verse:
The darkness tries to envelop me,
but The Light floods my soul.
Fingers of the past try to draw me back,
but love breaks their hold.

Chorus:
In Jesus name, there are no regrets
for God is in control.
In Jesus name there are no regrets
for in Him I am soundly sold.

Verse:
God took me out of such great darkness,
bringing me in His light.
He broke the chains that
bound me very tight,
giving me the key.

Chorus:
In Jesus name, there are no regrets
for God is in control.
In Jesus name there are no regrets
for in Him I am soundly sold.

Verse:
Things arose from the past I thought gone,
they Tried to drag me down,
For Jesus the Lamb of God took my sins,
and He made me whole.

Chorus:
In Jesus name, there are no regrets
for God is in control.
In Jesus name there are no regrets
for in Him I am soundly sold.

Bridge:
The pain of what might have been
rears its ugly head,
But God's voice whispering trust me
helps me to be bold instead,
He kept me with His Everlasting love
and healed the wounds within my soul.

Chorus:
In Jesus name, there are no regrets
for God is in control.
In Jesus name there are no regrets
for in Him I am soundly sold.

06. This Jordan

Verse:
I am looking to my God, up above,
Who has said, that He will never
leave me nor forsake me,
and I can do all things through
Christ, who strengthens me,
for only in Him am I able,
for only in Him am I set free,
he whom the Son sets free is free in deed.
free of this prison and the chains
that bound me until now.

Chorus:
I am determined, I have
purposed in my heart,
that I am crossing over this
Jordan that is facing me.

Verse:
For He has never left nor forsook me,
He has given me strength
when I truly needed it.
Jesus is My Rock, and He
is my awesome Lord,
and He is my More Than Enough God.
For in Him is no shadow of turning,
for He is the same now and forever.
and what He says I will rest in
because He does not lie.

Chorus:
I am determined, I have
purposed in my heart,
that I am crossing over this
Jordan that is facing me.

Verse:
I am looking to God, who is with me,
while searching God's word, I found,
seek Me and you shall find Me,
I can do all things through Christ,
who gives me strength,
for only in Him am I able,
for only in Him am I set free,
he whom the Son sets free is free in deed.
free of this prison and the chains
that bound me until now.

Chorus:
I am determined, I have
purposed in my heart,
that I am crossing over this
Jordan that is facing me.

Verse:
I am crying to my God, who hears me,
who has said, in His word, knock
and the door shall be opened,
and, I can do all things through
Christ, who strengthens me,
for only in Him am I able,
for only in Him am I set free,
he whom the Son sets free is free in deed.
to praise and worship giving
glory and honor to our God.

Chorus:
I am determined, I have
purposed in my heart,
that I am crossing over this
Jordan that is facing me.

07. This Path

Verse:
You set my feet on this path,
narrow is the way;
you set my feet on this path,
and here I am to stay.

Chorus:
You guide me, and lead me,
and show me the way,
every step of the way.

Verse:
You set my feet on this path,
from dark into light;
you set my feet on this path,
from death into true life.

Chorus:
You guide me, and lead me,
and show me the way,
every step of the way.

Verse:
You set my feet on this path,
hope is all around;
You set my feet on this path,
God's grace and peace abound.

Chorus:
You guide me, and lead me,
and show me the way,
every step of the way.

Verse:
You set my feet on this path,
and saved me from sin;
You set my feet on this path,
and your blood cleansed from sin.

Chorus:
You guide me, and lead me,
and show me the way,
every step of the way.

08. To Our God Most High

Chorus:
Let us give Glory, Honour and Praise,
to our God Most High,
let us give Glory, Honour and Praise,
to our God Most High.

Verse:
For You are The Rock on which we stand,
and the Air in which we breathe,
You are the shelter, under which we run,
and the Fortress into which we flee.

Chorus:
Let us give Glory, Honour and Praise,
to our God Most High,
let us give Glory, Honour and Praise,
to our God Most High.

Verse:
For You are The Life in which we live,
and The Way, that we should go,
You are The Light that does
brighten the way,
and The Truth that teaches us to know.

Chorus:
Let us give Glory, Honour and Praise,
to our God Most High,
let us give Glory, Honour and Praise,
to our God Most High.

Verse:
For You are Living Water, not dry,
and hears the heart when it cries,
You are The Shepherd, we choose to follow,
and The Word, of which we choose to read.

Chorus:
Let us give Glory, Honour and Praise,
to our God Most High,
let us give Glory, Honour and Praise,
to our God Most High.

Bridge:
Seek God's face and not His hands.
Choose God's holy way and not man's.
Rest in God's abiding arms
and find, hope, peace, love,
joy and strength.

Chorus:
Let us give Glory, Honour and Praise,
to our God Most High,
let us give Glory, Honour and Praise,
to our God Most High.

09. Jesus is The Light

Verse:
Come as you are, come as you are:
ragged and filthy, and broken of heart.
I've sent you a Light, come
out of the darkness,
I've sent you a Lamp, words to follow.
Walk in the Light and follow Lord Jesus,
walk in the Truth by reading God's word.

Chorus:
Jesus is The Lamp unto our feet,
and The Light unto our pathway,
and The Bright and Morning Star.
Jesus is The Truth, The Life, and The Way,
and The Word, that took on
flesh and dwelled among us.

Verse:
Come as you are, come as you are:
battered and shipwrecked,
and tossed to and fro.
I've sent you a Light, come
out of the darkness,
I've sent you a Lamp, words to follow.
Walk in the Light and follow Lord Jesus,
walk in the Truth by reading God's word.

Chorus:
Jesus is The Lamp unto our feet,
and The Light unto our pathway,
and The Bright and Morning Star.
Jesus is The Truth, The Life, and The Way,
and The Word, that took on
flesh and dwelled among us.

Verse:
Come as you are, come as you are:
empty and scared, and bruised to the bone.
I've sent you a Light, come
out of the darkness,
I've sent you a Lamp, words to follow.
Walk in the Light and follow Lord Jesus,
walk in the Truth by reading God's word.

Chorus:
Jesus is The Lamp unto our feet,
and The Light unto our pathway,
and The Bright and Morning Star.
Jesus is The Truth, The Life, and The Way,
and The Word, that took on
flesh and dwelled among us.

Chorus:
Jesus is The Lamp unto our feet,
and The Light unto our pathway,
and The Bright and Morning Star.
Jesus is The Truth, The Life, and The Way,
and The Word, that took on
flesh and dwelled among us.

10. Just Dare to Believe

Verse:
Can you see God? Look all around.
God's fingerprints are everywhere.
and if you will look, you will see.

Chorus:
Dare to believe, just dare to believe,
that God is God and Jesus is Lord,
Dare to believe, just dare to believe,
and accept His gift of life.
just dare to believe.

Bridge:
God The Father, God The Son,
and God The Holy Ghost,
all three in one, you see.

Chorus:
Dare to believe, just dare to believe,
that God is God and Jesus is Lord,
Dare to believe, just dare to believe,
and accept His gift of life.
just dare to believe.

Verse:
Will you accept God's Son, Jesus Christ?
let Him Be above all your Lord.
Jesus is knocking let Him in.

Chorus:
Dare to believe, just dare to believe,
that God is God and Jesus is Lord,
Dare to believe, just dare to believe,
and accept His gift of life.
just dare to believe.

11. Believe In Him

Verse:
It is true
that God loves you and me,
He proved it
on that old rugged tree.

Verse:
He is true,
in what He said and did,
The Lamb slain,
full of God's love, and grace.

Chorus:
The penalty for sin
was paid in full,
God's son hung upon that tree so cruel.
He died, was buried, and rose again,
Setting all free who truly do believe.

Verse:
Make this choice,
and accept Gods first Son,
you are; loved,
God has made it all known.

Chorus:
The penalty for sin
was paid in full,
God's son hung upon that tree so cruel.
He died, was buried, and rose again,
Setting all free who truly do believe.

Bridge:
God's Son Jesus Christ,
His only begotten son,
was the sacrificial Lamb of God,
who took my place and became sin for me,
through His death on that tree.

Chorus:
The penalty for sin
was paid in full,
God's son hung upon that tree so cruel.
He died, was buried, and rose again,
Setting all free who truly do believe.

12. Your Love

Verse:
God, Your love is a love that never changes,
from beginning to end
Your message is the same.

Chorus:
The greatest gift ever given to man,
is the love of God and His awesome plan.

Verse:
God, Your love is a love that never changes,
from beginning to end
Your message is the same.

Chorus:
The greatest gift ever given to man,
is the love of God and His awesome plan.

Bridge:
"For God so loved the world
that He gave His only begotten Son,
that who so ever believeth in Him
shall not perish, but have everlasting life,
and it more abundantly.

Chorus:
The greatest gift ever given to man,
is the love of God and His awesome plan.

13. Then One Day

Verse:
I set out on the road of life
a long, long time ago,
and like a ship on the sea
I was tossed about, to and fro.

Verse:
I groped my way down the lane blind,
but the void was unfilled,
look here-look there the voice cried,
one size fits all, no light just walls.

Chorus:
Then one day like a whisper on the wind
was, God so loved the world that He
gave His only begotten Son for all men.

Verse:
Still in darkness felt all around,
a light was up ahead,
for Jesus the Lamb of God
is the only true way, He said.

Chorus:
Then one day like a whisper on the wind
was, God so loved the world that He
gave His only begotten Son for all men.

Verse:
I stumbled out into the light,
my garment filled with stains,
but Jesus the Lamb of God,
took on himself all of my pain.

Chorus:
Then one day like a whisper on the wind
was, God so loved the world that He
gave His only begotten Son for all men.

Bridge:
I went up to the wooden cross,
and kneeled there at its base,
I looked upon Jesus Christ
the one who took my place.
He washed me clean from all my sins,
abide His word my heart within.
Jesus is the way, the truth and the life;
His word is a two edged sword, sharper
than any single edged knife.

Chorus:
Then one day like a whisper on the wind
was, God so loved the world that He
gave His only begotten Son for all men.

14. You Are With Me

Verse:
Though I, walk through the valley,
I shall not be afraid,
For You, my God, are with me.

Verse:
Though the waters surround me,
I shall trust in You Lord.
For You, my God, uphold me.

Chorus:
You are with me, every step of the way,
hid in You, here I am to stay,
yes, here I am to stay.

Verse:
Though I, walk through the fire,
I shall be hid in You.
For You, my God, protect me.

Verse:
Though the way be long and rough,
I shall hold Your hand,
For You, my God, strengthen me.

Chorus:
You are with me, every step of the way,
hid in You, here I am to stay,
yes, here I am to stay.

Verse:
Though I, trip, stumble or fall,
I shall get right back up.
For You, my God, do lift me.

Verse:
Though the fiery darts come,
They shall not do me harm,
For You, my God, do shield me.

Chorus:
You are with me, every step of the way,
hid in You, here I am to stay,
yes, here I am to stay.

Chorus:
You are with me, every step of the way,
hid in You, here I am to stay,
yes, here I am to stay.

15. God's Plan

Verse:
Through it all,
God made a way,
For after the fall,
man was born in sin.

Chorus:
Even before the world was made,
God's love made away,
and God's plan was for us
to come back to Him.
through Jesus Christ His Son.

Verse:
Through it all,
God had a plan,
for He sent His Son
to redeem all man.

Chorus:
Even before the world was made,
God's love made away,
and God's plan was for us
to come back to Him.
through Jesus Christ His Son.

Verse:
Through it all,
God's love is true,
He created us,
though we still choose.

Chorus:
Even before the world was made,
God's love made away,
and God's plan was for us
to come back to Him.
through Jesus Christ His Son.

Chorus:
Even before the world was made,
God's love made away,
and God's plan was for us
to come back to Him.
through Jesus Christ His Son.

16. *The Open Door*

Verse:
When the Jews rejected Him,
the door was open for me,
And when they led Him up the hill,
they nailed Him to a tree.
All the blood He shed;
He shed for you and me,
all the blood He shed;
He shed for you and me.

Verse:
They laid Him in a borrowed tomb,
it did look like death had won,
But then, early on the third day,
behold Jesus, Gods Son.
Jesus rose from the grave;
life was flowing through Him,
Jesus rose from the grave;
life was flowing through Him.

Verse:
Jesus Christ the Lamb of God,
who did shed His blood for thee,
won the battle o'er sin and death,
came forth in victory,
Who stands before God;
for all of you and me!
Who stands before God;
for all of you and me!

Verse:
When His word has been fulfilled,
before this old earth is done,
we are called to meet our Saviour,
while He is in the air.
Jesus Lord and Saviour,
comes to take us away.
Jesus Lord and Saviour,
comes to take us away.

17. Washed In The Blood Of The Lamb

Verse:

I am washed in the blood of the lamb-
In the blood of the precious Lamb of God.
I was spotted and stained deep within,
but now I'm made clean,
I was bound by sin,
but now I'm set free,
I am washed in the blood of the lamb-
In the blood of the precious Lamb of God.

Chorus:

Jesus blood was shed for me,
on a cruel, cruel tree,
He was the sacrificial Lamb of God,
who was led as a sheep to the slaughter,
and opened not His mouth.

Verse:

I am cleansed by the blood of the Lamb-
By the blood of the precious Lamb of God.
I was dead separated from God,
but now I'm in Thee.
I was blind to truth,
but now I can see.
I am cleansed by the blood of the Lamb-
By the blood of the precious Lamb of God.

Chorus:

Jesus blood was shed for me,
on a cruel, cruel tree,
He was the sacrificial Lamb of God,
who was led as a sheep to the slaughter,
and opened not His mouth.

Verse:

I am washed in the blood of the lamb-
In the blood of the precious Lamb of God.
I was spotted and stained deep within,
but now I'm made clean,
I was bound by sin,
but now I'm set free,
I am washed in the blood of the lamb-
In the blood of the precious Lamb of God.

Chorus:

Jesus blood was shed for me,
on a cruel, cruel tree,
He was the sacrificial Lamb of God,
who was led as a sheep to the slaughter,
and opened not His mouth.

18. Your Love Is

Verse:
Your Love,
is a banner over me.
Your Love,
has completely set me free.

Verse:
Your Light,
swallows up the total darkness.
Your Light,
was shed abroad in my heart.

Verse:
Your word,
Was Your love letter to read.
Your word,
Revealed our total need.

Verse:
Your Blood,
cleansed me from all my sin.
Your Blood,
was shed to set free all men.

Verse:
Your Life,
was given, as a life gift.
Your Life,
paid the price for sins rift.

Verse:
Your Love,
is a banner over me.
Your Love,
God who is Love set me free.

19. See

Pre-chorus:
Give us eyes to see,
You in everything,

Verse:
See the Lily of the valley,
see the sparrow fall,
see the lovely rose of Sharon,
And see how spring doth call.

Verse:
See the mountain up so high,
see the mighty oak,
see the river flowing by,
And see the fog and smoke.

Chorus:
Give us eyes to see,
You in everything,
seeing more of You,
our Creator in which we believe.

Verse:
See the stars up in the sky,
see the waterfall,
see the sands upon the beach,
And see He loves us all.

Verse:
See the rain that is falling down,
see the garden grow,
see the flowers of the field,
and see the lava flow.

Chorus:
Give us eyes to see,
You in everything,
seeing more of You,
our Creator in which we believe.

Verse:
see our Saviour on a tree,
see He shed blood for thee,
see He died and rose again,
And see we are free from sin.

Chorus:
Give us eyes to see,
You in everything,
seeing more of You,
our Creator in which we believe.

20. JESUS IS

Verse:
Jesus is Love,
love is the key,
that opens our heart.

Verse:
Jesus is Light,
the Lights a lamp,
unto our feet.

Chorus:
Jesus I look to You,
Jesus I love You,
Jesus, You are my everything, And all in all.

Verse:
Jesus is Lord,
Lord and Saviour,
of our soul.

Verse:
Jesus is King,
the King who sits,
upon His throne.

Chorus:
Jesus I look to You,
Jesus I love You,
Jesus, You are my everything, and all in all.

Verse:
Jesus is the Lamb,
the Lamb who shed,
His blood for thee.

Verse:
Jesus is god's Son,
who won o'er death,
victoriously.

Chorus:
Jesus I look to You,
Jesus I love You,
Jesus, You are my everything, and all in all.

21. UNITED WE STAND

Chorus:
United we stand,
divided we fall;
we need one another in the work
to which we are called.

Verse:
Hands holding hands,
helping one another
Each different from one another
none are the same,
but all working towards that
Glorious, glorious day.

Verse:
He comes again, and
gathers His body.
till that day when
we see His face, work in this place.
join the work in the field,
a good harvest has been revealed.

Chorus:
United we stand,
divided we fall;
we need one another in the work
to which we are called.

Chorus:
United we stand,
divided we fall;
we need one another in the work
to which we are called.

22. Born Again

Verse:
I live to worship You,
for my life is hid in You,
I can do all things through Christ Jesus,
who gives me strength,

Chorus:
The old has gone, the new is come,
I am born again,
old things have passed away,
behold all things have become new.
in our Lord Christ Jesus.

Verse:
I am my Lord God's child,
adopted in His family,
when I accepted Jesus Christ,
as Lord and Saviour,

Chorus:
The old has gone, the new is come,
I am born again,
old things have passed away,
behold all things have become new.
in our Lord Christ Jesus.

Verse:
I have been set free when,
repented of all my sins,
now a new creature in Christ Jesus.
rejoicing in Him.

Chorus:
The old has gone, the new is come,
I am born again,
old things have passed away,
behold all things have become new.
in our Lord Christ Jesus.

Bridge:
Faint not, fear not,
fret not, and put your trust in Him,
Tempt not, doubt not,
worry not, and rest in My peace
Fuss not, Lie not,
gossip not, and bridle your tongue.

Chorus:
The old has gone, the new is come,
I am born again,
old things have passed away,
behold all things have become new.
in our Lord Christ Jesus.

Section Two

Song Lyrics That Encourage

23. Always Nigh

Verse:
Down in the valley
or on a mountain top high,
we will look to Jesus,
who is always nigh.

Chorus:
Lift up your face and call on His name,
our Jesus Lord and Saviour is ever the same,
glory hallelujah blessed be His name,
our Jesus Lord and Saviour is ever the same.
lift up your hands and reverence His name,

Verse:
Through the stormy seas,
or walking the land shod dry,
I will look to Jesus,
who is always nigh,

Chorus:
Lift up your face and call on His name,
our Jesus Lord and Saviour is ever the same,
glory hallelujah blessed be His name,
our Jesus Lord and Saviour is ever the same.
lift up your hands and reverence His name,

Bridge:
Light or dark, day or night,
our Jesus Lord and Saviour,
is always nigh,
up or down, good or bad,
our Jesus Lord and Saviour
is by our side.

Chorus:
Lift up your face and call on His name,
our Jesus Lord and Saviour is ever the same,
glory hallelujah blessed be His name,
our Jesus Lord and Saviour is ever the same.
lift up your hands and reverence His name,

Verse:
Looking at the cross,
or that empty open tomb,
I will look to Jesus,
who is always nigh.

Chorus:
Lift up your face and call on His name,
our Jesus Lord and Saviour is ever the same,
glory hallelujah blessed be His name,
our Jesus Lord and Saviour is ever the same.
lift up your hands and reverence His name,

24. Just Hold on

Verse:
The valley is dark and deep,
just hold on,
God will carry you through.

Verse:
The walls close in and surround,
just hold on,
God will carry you through.

Chorus:
Don't give up,
don't give in,
don't give the enemy
any place.

Bridge:
Yea though I walk through,
the valley,
of the shadow of death
I will fear no evil,
for Thy rod and staff
they comfort me.

Chorus:
Don't give up,
don't give in,
don't give the enemy
any place.

Verse:
The waters try to overwhelm,
just hold on,
God will carry you through.

Chorus:
Don't give up,
don't give in,
don't give the enemy
any place.

Bridge:
My help cometh from the Lord.
who made heaven and earth,
the God of my salvation.

Chorus:
Don't give up,
don't give in,
don't give the enemy
any place.

25. Loved By Jesus

Verse:
The eagle flies into the sun;
Children laugh while having fun.
Seasons come and seasons go;
I hope one day that you will know,
you are loved by Jesus so.

Verse:
The river flows to the sea,
the rain falls on you and me,
seasons come and seasons go,
I hope one day that you will know,
that you're loved by Jesus so.

Chorus:
Tick tock goes the clock
from our birth to our death,
tick tock goes the clock,
for us to get to know,
that we are loved by Jesus so.

Verse:
The precious Lamb of God was slain,
cleansing all who do believe,
seasons come and seasons go,
I hope that one day you will know,
that you're loved by Jesus so.

Chorus:
Tick tock goes the clock
from our birth to our death,
tick tock goes the clock,
for us to get to know,
that we are loved by Jesus so.

26. Press in,

Verse:
Press in, to break through.
Push in, and hold on.
For the violent, take it by force.

Verse:
Press in, to break through.
Push in, and hold on.
For the violent, take it by force.

Chorus:
There is a crack,
a glimpse of light,
keep hammering away with God's word.
Force your way through.
Enlarge the hole,
let's make it big enough for travel.

Chorus:
There is a crack,
a glimpse of light,
keep hammering away with God's word.
Force your way through.
Enlarge the hole,
let's make it big enough for travel.

Bridge:
When changes come spiritually
for our break through,
it's not time to ease off, but press in,
it's not time to give up, but knuckle down,
it's not time to draw back,
but press through,
stand up, step out, and walk forward.

27. Hope In Jesus

Verse:
You have drawn me out of darkness,
into the marvelous light,
now standing at the throne in
the presence of my God,
falling at His feet, like dead but yet alive,
even in the darkness there is light,
now sitting with Jesus at our Fathers right.

Chorus:
There is hope in Jesus, all along the way,
there is hope in Jesus, who
turned night into day,
there is hope in Jesus, who
shed His blood for me,
there is hope in Jesus, who
set the captive free.

Verse:
Light the dark pathway with God's Word,
look to Jesus', death and rebirth,
the loving Shepherd Jesus,
God's sacrificial lamb,
who bore all on His shoulders,
the Great I Am,
so look to God, from wince comes our help.
Jesus Christ, God's only begotten son lives.

Chorus:
Put your hope in Jesus, all along the way,
put your hope in Jesus, who
turned night into day,
put your hope in Jesus, who
shed His blood for thee,
put your hope in Jesus, who
set the captive free.

Verse:
Look on our Lord, nailed on the tree,
who said if I'm lifted up,
I will draw all men to me, and
shedding His blood He died,
was buried and rose again for you and me,
to set all free who choose to believe,
who came forth in Victory and liberty.

Chorus:
So my hope is in Jesus, all along the way,
and my hope is in Jesus, who
turned night into day,
and my hope is in Jesus, who
shed His blood for me,
and my hope is in Jesus, who
set this captive free.

28. My Chosen Path

Verse:
I walked down the path till it became two,
I chose the narrow path, for it drew few.
step by step I go on this narrow path;
step by step I go looking not back.

Verse:
Though I find that this path isn't easy,
but neither is it hard, my Lord and
Saviour carried me, when I got tired.
Day by day I go with Him at my side;
day by day I go his word is my guide.

Chorus:
This is my chosen path,
to follow after You,
going forward, not back,
You Lord Jesus are my guide,
and never alone do I abide.

Verse:
Sometimes I'll rest along the
way, sometimes I run the race,
and sometimes things look dark,
clearly, not seeing His face.
Foot by foot I go, the day is done;
foot-by-foot, I go, the race is run.

Verse:
The light it shines upon my path,
darkness is driven back, come, Christ
is real, He has been revealed.
Piece by piece, I know, In Him, I am sealed;
piece-by-piece, I know, He is revealed.

Chorus:
This is my chosen path,
to follow after You,
going forward, not back,
You Lord Jesus are my guide,
and never alone do I abide.

Verse:
He makes me King and Priest on
High, Chosen of God am I, pressing
towards the mark, I hark.
Line by line, I know, His love is shown;
line by line, I know, Gods Son is known.

Chorus:
This is my chosen path,
to follow after You,
going forward, not back,
You Lord Jesus are my guide,
and never alone do I abide.

29. *The Broken Chains*

Verse:
I thought I knew my Lord and God;
but darkness filled my mind.
I thought I knew my Saviour's word;
most all I knew was lies.

Chorus:
He set me free, yes, He set me free,
He broke the chains that bound me,
praise God, He set me free.

Bridge:
Fear and ignorance, bondage and control,
was mostly all my mind did know.
before He set me free.

Chorus:
He set me free, yes, He set me free,
He broke the chains that bound me,
praise God, He set me free.

Verse:
One day my life began to change,
My Lord did rearrange.
The chains did break and I was free,
my Lord, He spoke to me.

Chorus:
He set me free, yes, He set me free,
He broke the chains that bound me,
praise God, He set me free.

Verse:
my soul was starved and very dry;
God, was for what it cried.
I love to praise His Holy Name;
Gods love's my glorious gain.

Chorus:
He set me free, yes, He set me free,
He broke the chains that bound me,
praise God, He set me free.

Verse:
There are people who lead us astray;
we forgive them and pray.
That their souls I will forgive;
and Gods love in them live.

Chorus:
He set me free, yes, He set me free,
He broke the chains that bound me,
praise God, He set me free.

30. *Which One?*

Verse:
This road I am on it leads to two,
which one will you follow?
The one called truth or the other lies,
which one can you swallow?

Verse:
This road I am on it leads to two,
which one can you see?
The one called light or the other dark,
which one will set you free?

Chorus:
I've set out on a road,
a road that leads to two,
I have to make a choice,
so which one do I choose.

Verse:
This road I am on it leads to two,
which one can you walk?
The one called narrow or other wide,
which one leads to the rock

Chorus:
I've set out on a road,
a road that leads to two,
I have to make a choice,
so which one do I choose.

Bridge:
I choose Truth,
I choose Light,
I choose the straight and Narrow Path,
Yes, God, I choose You.

Chorus:
I've set out on a road,
a road that leads to two,
I have to make a choice,
so which one do I choose.

Tag:
God, I choose You,
I choose You,
I choose You,
Yes, God, I choose You.

31. BATTLES

Verse:
I stood upon a mountain high
contemplating times gone bye.
The battles on that mountain top,
of those who won and those who lost.

Verse:
It was not very long ago,
I found a battle also.
One of hopelessness, one of despair,
one of darkness, not wanting there.

Chorus:
God the Father-God the Son,
God the Holy Spirit three in one.
Now I follow truth and light,
for in God is hope, love, joy and life.

Bridge: I felt as if I would drown
in all the troubles that were around.
Crying O' God help me I pray,
I don't know what to do, I need You today.
I need You, for everything.

Chorus:
God the Father-God the Son,
God the Holy Spirit three in one.
Now I follow truth and light,
for in God is hope, love, joy and life.

Verse:
The ball and chain that held me fast,
God unlocked setting me free.
To walk in the marvelous light,
being led by my Lord Jesus.

Chorus:
God the Father-God the Son,
God the Holy Spirit three in one.
Now I follow truth and light,
for in God is hope, love, joy and life.

Verse:
I held God's hand and held it tight.
He broke the chains and loosed me,
His loving arms surrounded me.
my awesome God, I praise Thee.

Chorus:
God the Father-God the Son,
God the Holy Spirit three in one.
Now I follow truth and light,
for in God is hope, love, joy and life.

32. Believe and Receive

Verse:
He sent His word and it healed them.
By His stripes we are healed.
Jesus is here to heal us,
He boar all our sicknesses,
diseases, and infirmities.
The prayer of Faith has healed me,
by faith I am healed.

Chorus:
God says, believe,
by Jesus' stripes, I am healed,
Lord, I believe.
God says, receive,
accept what has already been done,
Lord, I receive.

Verse:
All those who came to Him and believed,
He healed by touching them,
or by a spoken word,
Lord Jesus only did what He
saw His Father God do.
He sets free all who are His and are,
oppressed and bound, by faith.

Chorus:
God says, believe,
by Jesus' stripes, I am healed,
Lord, I believe.
God says, receive,
accept what has already been done,
Lord, I receive.

Bridge:
Heal me, and I am healed.
God has healed me,
Through Jesus, and I am healed.

Chorus:
God says, believe,
by Jesus' stripes, I am healed,
Lord, I believe.
God says, receive,
accept what has already been done,
Lord, I receive.

Chorus:
God says, believe,
by Jesus' stripes, I am healed,
Lord, I believe.
God says, receive,
accept what has already been done,
Lord, I receive.

33. We Rise Up

Verse:
Life's road seems trying and hard,
stumbling and falling,
We rise up,
and continue to follow the Light.

Verse:
Life's storms try to overthrow,
battering and pummeling,
we steadfast,
and continue to hold to the Rock.

Chorus:
The Light is God's word,
He is a lamp unto our feet,
and a Light unto our pathway,
The Rock is God's son,
The Rock Christ Jesus, Almighty,
on which we stand steadfast in Him.

Bridge:
We rise up,
we steadfast,
we hold tight,
and look not back.

Chorus:
The Light is God's word,
He is a lamp unto our feet,
and a Light unto our pathway,
The Rock is God's son,
The Rock Christ Jesus, Almighty,
on which we stand steadfast in Him.

34. It's Okay

Verse:
In those times we feel all alone,
hold fast and cling tight,
to life and light in God's word,
We are never left alone, nor,
are we forsaken.

Verse:
In those times we seem to be lost,
steadfast, and take your stand,
to direction in God's word.
We may plan the way we go, but,
our God orders our steps.

Chorus:
In those times we have no hope,
latch hold, and don't let go,
to believe what God's word says.
Be joyful in hope, patient in,
affliction, faithful in prayer.

Chorus:
In those times we have no hope,
latch hold, and don't let go,
to believe what God's word says.
Be joyful in hope, patient in,
affliction, faithful in prayer.

Bridge:
He who has begun a good work in us,
is able to complete it.
Abide in Me, and I in you,
for apart from Me, you can do nothing.
Look to God, lean on Him,
rest in God and trust in Him,
God will turn what was
meant for evil to good.

Chorus:
In those times we have no hope,
latch hold, and don't let go,
to believe what God's word says.
Be joyful in hope, patient in,
affliction, faithful in prayer.

35. *The Word*

Verse:
Don't look back, move on ahead,
you are not alone.

Chorus:
Jesus said, He'd never leave us,
nor forsake us,
He's not a man that He should lie,
let every man be a liar,
but, Christ Jesus is true.

Verse:
Make a choice, to take each step,
one step at a time.

Chorus:
Jesus said, He'd never leave us,
nor forsake us,
He's not a man that He should lie,
let every man be a liar,
but, Christ Jesus is true.

Verse:
Hold to the Word, and be assured,
in Jesus's name, God hears.

Chorus:
Jesus said, He'd never leave us,
nor forsake us,
He's not a man that He should lie,
let every man be a liar,
but, Christ Jesus is true.

Bridge:
The Word was with God,
The Word was God,
The Word took on flesh,
and dwelled among us.

Chorus:
Jesus said, He'd never leave us,
nor forsake us,
He's not a man that He should lie,
let every man be a liar,
but, Christ Jesus is true.

36. Cling To The Rock

Pre-Chorus:
Cling to The Rock,
The Rock Christ Jesus.

Chorus:
Do not let go,
hold on with all your might,
and cling to the Rock,
The Rock Christ Jesus.

Verse:
When the storms try to overthrow,
I choose to cling to The Rock,
The Rock Christ Jesus,
and never let go.

Verse:
Waters try to envelop me,
I choose to see Christ Jesus,
The Rock Christ Jesus,
not on the troubles.

Pre-Chorus:
Cling to The Rock,
The Rock Christ Jesus.

Chorus:
Do not let go,
hold on with all your might,
and cling to the Rock,
The Rock Christ Jesus.

Verse:
When the ground shakes under your feet,
stand on The Rock Christ Jesus,
steadfast and quite sure,
God is in control.

Bridge: Jesus is The Rock,
an anchor to my soul,
Jesus is The Rock,
The Rock Christ Jesus,
to whom I'll never let go.

Pre-Chorus:
Cling to The Rock,
The Rock Christ Jesus.

Chorus:
Do not let go,
hold on with all your might,
and cling to the Rock,
The Rock Christ Jesus.

37. Not Our Battle

Verse:
Be strong, courageous, and firm,
strong, courageous, and firm,
when crossing over the Jordan
that is set before you.

Verse:
Be strong, courageous, and firm,
strong, courageous, and firm,
when you are facing the giants,
that try to slay you.

Chorus:
We are not alone,
our God has gone before us,
the battle is not ours,
for it is the Lord's,
if God is for us,
who can be against us.

Verse:
Be strong, courageous, and firm,
strong, courageous, and firm,
for when the world walks in darkness,
we walk in our God's light.

Chorus:
We are not alone,
our God has gone before us,
the battle is not ours,
for it is the Lord's,
if God is for us,
who can be against us.

Bridge:
Be strong, be courageous, be firm,
in the Lord God, the light of the world.

Chorus:
We are not alone,
our God has gone before us,
the battle is not ours,
for it is the Lord's,
if God is for us,
who can be against us.

Chorus:
We are not alone,
our God has gone before us,
the battle is not ours,
for it is the Lord's,
if God is for us,
who can be against us.

38. In The Palm of Your Hand

Verse:
You are not alone,
the Lord God Almighty,
is with you.

Verse:
You are not abandoned,
the Lord God Almighty
is in you.

Chorus:
We are in the palm
of Your hand O' God,
we are on Your mind
both day and night.

Verse:
You are not forsaken,
the Lord God Almighty,
is holding you.

Chorus:
We are in the palm
of Your hand O' God,
we are on Your mind
both day and night.

Verse:
You are not forgotten,
the Lord God Almighty,
is guiding you.

Chorus:
We are in the palm
of Your hand O' God,
we are on Your mind
both day and night.

Verse:
You are not alone,
the Lord God Almighty,
is with you.

Chorus:
We are in the palm
of Your hand O' God,
we are on Your mind
both day and night.

39. None Like God

Verse:
God's ways are perfect,
He is the rock,
for all His ways are law and justice,
and O so faithful,
to all those He has called and chosen.

Verse:
God's work is perfect,
His Son our salvation,
and none are delivered out of His hand,
revenging Himself
against the blood of His servants,

Chorus:
There is none like God,
who rides through the heavens to our help,
in His majestic glory, through the skies.
He is our refuge and dwelling place,
and underneath are His everlasting arms,
ever going before us,
thrusting out our enemies.

Verse:
God's word is perfect.
dwelling in safety,
we rejoice in His holy name,
for He is our help
in our time of trouble.

Chorus:
There is none like God,
who rides through the heavens to our help,
in His majestic glory, through the skies.
He is our refuge and dwelling place,
and underneath are His everlasting arms,
ever going before us,
thrusting out our enemies.

Bridge:
God is perfect, His ways are perfect,
His work is perfect, His word is perfect,
God Almighty is perfect.

Chorus:
There is none like God,
who rides through the heavens to our help,
in His majestic glory, through the skies.
He is our refuge and dwelling place,
and underneath are His everlasting arms,
ever going before us,
thrusting out our enemies.

40. Through It All

Verse:
The storms they try to overthrow,
but in Jesus' name,
say, peace be still,
for the Prince of Peace is here.

Chorus:
Through it all no matter what,
remain in God's strong arms,
cradled in His loving embrace,
yes, no matter what, through it all.

Verse:
The battle rages all around,
and in Jesus' name,
say, I rebuke you satan,
for the battle is the Lord's.

Chorus:
Through it all no matter what,
remain in God's strong arms,
cradled in His loving embrace,
yes, no matter what, through it all.

Bridge:
Through it all, whatever may come,
we are safely secure,
in our Lord,
through it all, no matter what,
comes our way.

Chorus:
Through it all no matter what,
remain in God's strong arms,
cradled in His loving embrace,
yes, no matter what, through it all.

Verse:
Even though everyone has left utterly,
yet in Jesus' name,
say, I am not alone,
for God is with me.

Chorus:
Through it all no matter what,
remain in God's strong arms,
cradled in His loving embrace,
yes, no matter what, through it all.

41. Written In Your Word

Verse:
You Lord, turned the water into wine,
taking nothing making it something,
speaking it into existence,
there is nothing too hard for
You, if we will only believe.

Verse:
You multiplied the fishes and loaves,
when a young boy shared his simple lunch,
making much from the little offered,
looking to Your Father above,
neither surprised nor doubting.

Chorus:
Lord we believe, You have
said it, and it is done,
as it is written in Your word,
for us to read.

Verse:
You came down to this
earth clothed as man,
Behold God's lamb, who takes away
all sins, being set free in Him alone,
choose life in God through Christ
Jesus, and follow Father God's plan.

Chorus:
Lord we believe, You have
said it, and it is done,
as it is written in Your word,
for us to read.

First Bridge:
Increase our faith,
open our eyes,
to see You more clearly,
we need You, to know You,
through Your written word.

Chorus:
Lord we believe, You have
said it, and it is done,
as it is written in Your word,
for us to read.

Second Bridge:
As it is written,
as it is written,
in Your Holy Word.
As it is written,
as it is written,
in Your precious word.
As it is written,
as it is written,
in Your life-giving Word.

Chorus:
Lord we believe, You have
said it, and it is done,
as it is written in Your word,
for us to read.

42. Victory Is Here

Pre-Chorus:
Your victory is here,
just reach out and believe.

Chorus:
Jesus is our victory,
our victory is in the Lord,
Jesus is our victory,
it has already been prepared.

Verse:
Like the woman with the issue of blood,
she reached out and believed,
and by her faith she was made whole.

Verse:
Like the lame man sitting beside the gate,
he stood up and began to leap,
for his faith set him free.

Pre-Chorus:
Your victory is here,
just reach out and believe.

Chorus:
Jesus is our victory,
our victory is in the Lord,
Jesus is our victory,
it has already been prepared.

Bridge:
Trust in God, in Jesus' name,
just believe, and you shall see,
your victory is here.

Pre-Chorus:
Your victory is here,
just reach out and believe.

Chorus:
Jesus is our victory,
our victory is in the Lord,
Jesus is our victory,
it has already been prepared.

Tag:
it's here, just believe,
And you'll see,
Victory in Christ Jesus,
Victory in the Lord.

43. In Him Alone

Verse:
Be ye filled with,
love, joy, and peace,
life, power, and hope,
from Christ Jesus.

Verse:
Yes walk there in,
love, joy, and peace,
life, power, and hope,
in Christ Jesus.

Chorus:
We walk in love empowered by our Lord,
we walk in joy as His overcomers,
we walk in peace that passes
all understanding,
we walk in life and it more abundantly,
we walk in power by His Might,
we walk in hope everlasting,
in Him alone.

Verse:
Stay steadfast in,
love, joy, and peace,
life, power, and hope,
through Christ Jesus.

Chorus:
We walk in love empowered by our Lord,
we walk in joy as His overcomers,
we walk in peace that passes
all understanding,
we walk in life and it more abundantly,
we walk in power by His Might,
we walk in hope everlasting,
in Him alone.

Bridge:
True life is in Christ Jesus
the Saviour of our soul,
without Him we have nothing good,
no love, joy, and peace,
no life, power, and hope,
but with Him we have life,
and it more abundantly.

Chorus:
We walk in love empowered by our Lord,
we walk in joy as His overcomers,
we walk in peace that passes
all understanding,
we walk in life and it more abundantly,
we walk in power by His Might,
we walk in hope everlasting,
in Him alone.

44. Time

Verse:
Now is the time for salvation,
now is the time to make Jesus Lord,
now is the time to walk in your calling,
now is the time to focus forward.

Verse:
Now is the time to follow the Shepherd,
now is the time to seek God's face,
now is the time to die out to self,
now is the time to run the race.

Chorus:
Now is the time, there is no time to waste,
now is the time, except God's Son,
now is the time,
now is the time.

Verse:
Now is the time to choose death or life,
now is the time to walk in light,
now is the time to find your purpose,
now is the time to stand for what's right.

Chorus:
Now is the time, there is no time to waste,
now is the time, except God's Son,
now is the time,
now is the time.

Bridge 1:
What are you waiting for,
why do you delay,
now is the time,
Lord Jesus bids come.

Chorus:
Now is the time, there is no time to waste,
now is the time, except God's Son,
now is the time,
now is the time.

Bridge 2:
This is the time, there is no
more time to waste,
this is the time, seek God
through Christ Jesus,
and walk in His grace.

Chorus:
Now is the time, there is no time to waste,
now is the time, except God's Son,
now is the time,
now is the time.

45. For Keeps

Chorus:
This is for keeps, this is for all or nothing,
this is for the high calling of God
in Christ Jesus our Lord.

Verse:
All the signs point the way,
all is made clear,
Jesus Christ is coming back,
be one for which He is here.

Tag:
Jesus Christ is coming back,
be one for which He is here.
Be one for which He is here.

Chorus:
This is for keeps, this is for all or nothing,
this is for the high calling of God
in Christ Jesus our Lord.

Verse:
All the signs point the way,
all is made clear,
Jesus Christ is coming back,
be one for which He is here.

Chorus:
This is for keeps, this is for all or nothing,
this is for the high calling of God
in Christ Jesus our Lord.

Bridge:
No time to waste, no time to play,
no time to give up, no time to delay.

Chorus:
This is for keeps, this is for all or nothing,
this is for the high calling of God
in Christ Jesus our Lord.

Verse:
All the signs point the way,
all is made clear,
Jesus Christ is coming back,
be one for which He is here.

Chorus:
This is for keeps,
this is for all or nothing,
this is for the high calling of God
in Christ Jesus our Lord.

46. Waiting

Verse:
Call upon the Lord,
seek Him while He may be found,
not to settle for less,
but to know all of Him.

Chorus:
The Lord is standing by,
waiting for you to call,
the Lord is standing by,
seek and ye shall find.

Verse:
Wait upon the Lord,
and He will renew your strength,
never settle for less,
to know Him is the best.

Chorus:
The Lord is standing by,
waiting for you to call,
the Lord is standing by,
seek and ye shall find.

Verse:
Rest upon the Lord,
for we are made strong in Him,
do not settle for less,
to know Him is great joy.

Chorus:
The Lord is standing by,
waiting for you to call,
the Lord is standing by,
seek and ye shall find.

Bridge:
He is waiting, waiting with open arms,
He is waiting, waiting for
you to call on Him,
He is waiting, waiting for you to knock,
He is waiting, waiting to open the door.

Chorus:
The Lord is standing by,
waiting for you to call,
the Lord is standing by,
seek and ye shall find.

Tag:
He is waiting,
He is waiting,
He is waiting,
waiting for you.

47. Come and Follow Me

Verse:
Though the road be rough and
rocky Jesus will lead us through,
though the waters are over our
heads Jesus will lead us through.

Verse:
Though the path is hard to see
Jesus will guide us through,
though we walk in the valley so dark
Jesus will guide us through.

Chorus:
Through it all Jesus leads,
through it all Jesus guides,
through it all Jesus supplies,
through it all Jesus beckons,
come and follow Me.
come and follow Me My beloved, come
and follow Me My dearest child,
come, and follow Me, with every
step you take, come, and follow Me,
through each and every day,
come and follow Me, all the way.

Verse:
Though we are totally unable Jesus
will supply all of our needs,
though everything has been lost
Jesus will supply all of our needs.

Verse:
Though we are weary in life
Jesus will beckon us on,
though we are sorely tried
Jesus will beckon us on.

Chorus
Through it all Jesus leads,
through it all Jesus guides,
through it all Jesus supplies,
through it all Jesus beckons,
come and follow Me.
come and follow Me My beloved, come
and follow Me My dearest child,
come, and follow Me, with every
step you take, come, and follow Me,
through each and every day,
come and follow Me, all the way.

Bridge:
Come and follow Me and I
will lead you through,
come and follow Me and I
will guide your way,
come and follow Me and I
will supply all needs,
come and follow Me and I
will beckon you on.
come, and follow Me.

Chorus:
Through it all Jesus leads,
through it all Jesus guides,
through it all Jesus supplies,
through it all Jesus beckons,
come and follow Me.
come and follow Me My beloved, come
and follow Me My dearest child,
come, and follow Me, with every
step you take, come, and follow Me,
through each and every day,
come and follow Me, all the way.

48. Come, Let's Go

Verse:
Open your mouth and speak God's Word,
it's time to take a stand,
lining up not breaking rank.
Lead us Lord, for we are God's Army,
and march as one in Christ,
led by the Holy Spirit true and right.

Chorus:
Listen, don't you hear the call?
Harkin to the sound of battle,
hear our Lord saying,
come, let's go, it's time to take
your stand and fight.

Bridge:
Lord, You are our Shield, and buckler,
our Rock, and our Defense,
our Fortress, and our Strong Tower,
into which we can run.

Chorus:
Listen, don't you hear the call?
Harkin to the sound of battle,
hear our Lord saying,
come, let's go, it's time to take
your stand and fight.

Verse:
the battle is the Lord Christ Jesus',
for in Him, we are seated,
therefore, VICTORY is ours.
Victorious in Christ Jesus,
Running to the battle,
God making what is wrong right in Christ.

Chorus:
Listen, don't you hear the call?
Harkin to the sound of battle,
hear our Lord saying,
come, let's go, it's time to take
your stand and fight.

49. God is Real, God is True (Possibly a Rap).

Chorus:
Believe in god, believe in God's word,
He does not change, and He
is forever the same.

Verse:
Healing is mine as God's child,
I am the healed of the Lord,
taking out cancer with God's word.
Jesus Christ said, that healing
is the children's bread,
and by His stripes I am healed,
Yes this is God's will,
despite what satan tries to get us to believe.

Verse:
In God all my needs are met, and
even some of my desires,
what I put my hands to prospers.
Prosper and be in health even
as your soul prospers,
Lord God is the Way-Maker,
and He doesn't lie,
let every man be a liar, but God is true.

Chorus:
Believe in god, believe in God's word,
He does not change, and He
is forever the same.

Bridge:
God is real, God is true, open
your eyes and see the proof.
The stars above, the earth below,
what more is needed to see it so?

Chorus:
Believe in god, believe in God's word,
He does not change, and He
is forever the same.

Verse:
The word says, we are God's children,
and precious in His sight,
We are joint heirs with Christ Jesus,
I am the righteousness of God in Jesus,
and the apple of His eye,
a sheep of His fold,
more precious than gold.

Verse:
Father God created us, and
Jesus Christ is the Word,
God is Father-Jesus is Son.
Commit totally to the King
and let Him reign,
as Lord over all will and plan,
and walk in VICTORY,
all across this land.

Chorus:
Believe in god, believe in God's word,
He does not change, and He
is forever the same.

Section Three

End-time Song Lyrics

50. *What a day that will be*

Verse:
Pour out Your Spirit upon all flesh O God,
and Let our sons and daughters prophecy.

Verse:
Pour out Your Spirit upon all flesh O God,
old men see dreams and
young men see visions.

Chorus:
What a day, that will be,
when our Saviour, we shall see,
when He comes back in the clouds,
and we hear the trumpet sound,
Glory hallelujah, Praises to our King

Verse:
Pour out Your Spirit upon all flesh O God,
among servants and the handmaidens too.

Chorus:
What a day, that will be,
when our Saviour, we shall see,
when He comes back in the clouds,
and we hear the trumpet sound,
Glory hallelujah, Praises to our King

Verse:
Pour out Your Spirit upon all flesh O God,
and show wonders on high
and on the earth.

Chorus:
What a day, that will be,
when our Saviour, we shall see,
when He comes back in the clouds,
and we hear the trumpet sound,
Glory hallelujah, Praises to our King

Verse:
Pour out Your Spirit upon all flesh O God,
and show us blood, fire and
pillars of smoke.

Chorus:
What a day, that will be,
when our Saviour, we shall see,
when He comes back in the clouds,
and we hear the trumpet sound,
Glory hallelujah, Praises to our King

Chorus:
What a day, that will be,
when our Saviour, we shall see,
when He comes back in the clouds,
and we hear the trumpet sound,
Glory hallelujah, Praises to our King

51. Call On Jesus

Verse:
The Great and Terrible Day of
The Lord will come to man.
The Great and Terrible day of
The Lord will come to man.
The sun shall cease to shine; the
moon shall turn to blood.
The Great and Terrible Day of
The Lord will come to man.

Chorus1:
But if ye call on Jesus, ye shall be delivered.
But if ye call on Jesus, ye shall be saved.
Yes if ye call on Jesus, ye shall be delivered.
Yes if ye call on Jesus, ye shall be saved.

Verse:
The Great and Terrible Day of
The Lord is come to man.
The Great and Terrible Day of
The Lord is come to man.
The sun shall cease to shine; the
moon shall turn to blood.
The Great and Terrible Day of
The Lord is come to man.

Chorus2:
But if ye call on Jesus, ye shall be delivered.
But if ye call on Jesus, ye shall be saved.
Yes if ye call on Jesus, ye shall be delivered.
Yes if ye call on Jesus, ye shall be saved.

Verse:
The Great and Terrible Day of
The Lord has come to man.
The Great and Terrible Day of
The Lord has come to man.
The sun has ceased to shine; the
moon has turned to blood.
The Great and Terrible Day of
The Lord has come to man.

Chorus3:
And if ye'd called on Jesus,
ye'd been delivered.
And if ye'd called on Jesus, ye'd been saved.
Yes if ye'd called on Jesus,
ye'd been delivered.
Yes if ye'd called on Jesus, ye'd been saved.

52. Come Lord Jesus

Chorus:
I come speedily,
I come quickly,
swiftly I come to you,
swiftly I come.

Verse:
I am the root, and the source,
and the offspring of David,
the radiant and brilliant morning star.

Verse:
I am the Alpha and Omega,
the First and the Last,
and the Before All and End of All.

Chorus:
I come speedily,
I come quickly,
swiftly I come to you,
swiftly I come.

Verse:
Behold I Am coming soon,
and I shall bring My wages
and rewards with Me, to repay and render.

Chorus:
I come speedily,
I come quickly,
swiftly I come to you,
swiftly I come.

Bridge:
Come Lord Jesus,
come we pray,
come Lord Jesus,
come we say,
Your children cry come.

Chorus:
I come speedily,
I come quickly,
swiftly I come to you,
swiftly I come.

Chorus:
I come speedily,
I come quickly,
swiftly I come to you,
swiftly I come.

53. Watch and Wait

Chorus:
Look up, watch and wait,
for just as the lightning flashes from the
east, shines and is seen, as far as the west,
so will the coming, of the Son of man be.

Verse:
Sky and earth will pass away, but
His word will not pass away,
but of that exact day and
hour no one knows,
not even the angels of Heaven, nor
the Son, only our Heavenly Father.

Verse:
As in the day of Noah, so is
the coming of Jesus,
for just as in those days
before the flood came,
they did not know nor understand, until
the flood came and swept them all away.

Chorus:
Look up, watch and wait,
for just as the lightning flashes from the
east, shines and is seen, as far as the west,
so will the coming, of the Son of man be.

Verse:
After the tribulation, comes the
sign of the Son of man,
appears in the sky and all
the tribes of the earth,
will mourn and lament in anguish, to see
Him coming on the clouds in great glory.

Chorus:
Look up, watch and wait,
for just as the lightning flashes from the
east, shines and is seen, as far as the west,
so will the coming, of the Son of man be.

Verse:
Sending out His angels with a loud
trumpet call, to gather all of His elect,
His chosen ones even from the four winds,
and even from one end of the -
universe to the other end of it.

Chorus:
Look up, watch and wait,
for just as the lightning flashes from the
east, shines and is seen, as far as the west,
so will the coming, of the Son of man be.

Bridge:
He is coming, we know not when,
but He is coming.

Chorus:
Look up, watch and wait,
for just as the lightning flashes from the
east, shines and is seen, as far as the west,
so will the coming, of the Son of man be.

54. We Eagerly Wait

Chorus:
Come Lord Jesus,
come what may,
come Lord Jesus,
we eagerly wait.

Verse:
All creation groans for Your return,
how much longer do we have to wait,
how much longer do we
remain in this state?

Verse:
All true children of God cry Lord come,
this present world is not our true home,
even the tomb didn't stop You
though blocked by a stone.

Chorus:
Come Lord Jesus,
come what may,
come Lord Jesus,
we eagerly wait.

Verse:
All power is in Your nail scared hands,
we look to You Jesus Christ our Lord,
in which out of whose mouth
comes a two edged sword.

Verse:
All tongues will confess Jesus Christ Lord,
every knee shall bow and reverence You,
God's Almighty Son as
Lord of lords so true.

Chorus:
Come Lord Jesus,
come what may,
come Lord Jesus,
we eagerly wait.

Chorus:
Come Lord Jesus,
come what may,
come Lord Jesus,
we eagerly wait.

Section Four

Song Lyrics Full Of Joy

55. You Are

Chorus:
Let us give glory, honor, and praise
to You, Our God Most High.
Let us give glory, honor, and praise
to You, Our God Most High.

Verse:
You are the Rock on which we stand,
and the air in which we breathe.
You are the shelter under which we run,
and the fortress into which we flee.

Chorus:
Let us give glory, honor, and praise
to You, Our God Most High.
Let us give glory, honor, and praise
to You, Our God Most High.

Verse:
For you are the life we do live,
and the way we know to go.
for You are the light that brightens the way,
and are the Truth that teaches to know.

Chorus:
Let us give glory, honor, and praise
to You, Our God Most High.
Let us give glory, honor, and praise
to You, Our God Most High.

Verse:
You are needed living water,
who hears the heart when it cries.
You are the Shepherd we choose to follow,
And in whom we do abide.

Chorus:
Let us give glory, honor, and praise
to You, Our God Most High.
Let us give glory, honor, and praise
to You, Our God Most High.

Bridge:
So we give Our God Most High
all the Glory, honor, and praise.
Gladly we give Our God Most High
all the glory, honor, and praise,
for the rest of our days.

Chorus:
Let us give glory, honor, and praise
to You, Our God Most High.
Let us give glory, honor, and praise
to You, Our God Most High.

56. The Rock Christ Jesus

Verse:
Standing on the Rock Christ Jesus,
the stone the builders disallowed.
Standing on the Rock Christ Jesus,
look at where He is now.

Verse:
Standing on the Rock Christ Jesus,
no storm nor no wave shall bring low.
Standing on the Rock Christ Jesus,
secure in all we know.

Chorus:
We are standing,
we are standing,
we are standing on the Rock Christ Jesus.
We are standing,
we are standing,
we are standing on the Rock Christ Jesus.

Verse:
Standing on the Rock Christ Jesus,
rooted and grounded here to stay.
Standing on the Rock Christ Jesus,
His life for us He paid.

Chorus:
We are standing,
we are standing,
we are standing on the Rock Christ Jesus.
We are standing,
we are standing,
we are standing on the Rock Christ Jesus.

Chorus:
We are standing,
We are standing,
We are standing on the Rock Christ Jesus.
We are standing,
We are standing,
We are standing on the Rock Christ Jesus.

57. That Name

Verse:
What a life giving name,
What a hope filled name,
What power is in that wonderful name.

Chorus:
That name is Christ Jesus,
God's Only Begotten Son,
That name is The Head Shepherd,
and The Sacrificial Lamb of God.
That name is The bride groom,
and The Bright and Morning Star,

Verse:
What a Joy giving name,
What a Love filled name,
What Might is in that wonderful name.

Chorus:
That name is Christ Jesus,
God's Only Begotten Son,
That name is The Head Shepherd,
and The Sacrificial Lamb of God.
That name is The bride groom,
and The Bright and Morning Star,

Verse:
What a Peace giving name,
What a Healing name,
What Strength is in that wonderful name.

Chorus:
That name is Christ Jesus,
God's Only Begotten Son,
That name is The Head Shepherd,
and The Sacrificial Lamb of God.
That name is The bride groom,
and The Bright and Morning Star,

Chorus:
That name is Christ Jesus,
God's Only Begotten Son,
That name is The Head Shepherd,
and The Sacrificial Lamb of God.
That name is The bride groom,
and The Bright and Morning Star,

58. Blessed

Chorus:
Blessed is the Lord,
and blessed is His name,
and blessed are His people.

Verse:
He shall feed His sheep,
and lead us all to drink,
and Deliver us from evil.

Verse:
Light is all around,,
hope doth abound,
and joy fills His people.

Chorus:
Blessed is the Lord,
and blessed is His name,
and blessed are His people.

Chorus:
Blessed is the Lord,
and blessed is His name,
and blessed are His people.

59. The Shepher's Sheep?

Verse:
Come to the well that never runs dry,
never runs dry, never runs dry,
come to the well that never runs
dry and never thirst again.

Verse:
Feed in the pasture lush and green,
lush and green, lush and green,
feed in the pasture lush and green
with what's set before you.

Verse:
Hear the Shepherd call His sheep,
call His sheep, call His sheep,
hear the Shepherd call His sheep
and bring them in the fold.

Verse:
See Him count them one by one,
one by one, one by one,
see Him count them one by one
to see that none are lost.

Verse:
He leaves the ninety-nine to find the
one, to find the one, to find the one,
He leaves the ninety-nine to find the
one, and hunts it high and low.

Verse:
Hallelujah I found my sheep, I found
my sheep, I found my sheep,
hallelujah I found my sheep,
rejoicing on the way home.

60. In This House

Verse:
Let there be; peace, peace, peace of God,
in this house,
let there be; peace, peace, peace of God,
in this house,
let there be; peace, peace, peace of God,
in this house,
for thou O' God are the
Prince of Peace indeed.

Verse:
Let there be; rest, rest, rest of God,
in this house,
let there be; rest, rest, rest of God,
in this house,
let there be; rest, rest, rest of God,
in this house,
for thou O' God do hold me in Your hand.

Verse:
Let there be; love, love, love of God,
in this house,
let there be; love, love, love of God,
in this house,
let there be; love, love, love of God,
in this house,
for thou O' God are love
and first Loved me.

Verse:
Let there be; joy, joy, joy of God,
in this house,
let there be; joy, joy, joy of God,
in this house,
let there be; joy, joy, joy of God,
in this house,
for thou O' God I rejoiceth to see.

Verse:
Let there be; need, need, need of God,
in this house,
let there be; need, need, need of God,
in this house,
let there be; need, need, need of God,
in this house,
for thou O' God set the captives free.

61. Praise Ye Jehovah

Verse:
Praise ye the Lord,
praise ye Jehovah,
praise ye the Lord,
praise Your Holy Name.

Verse:
Rejoice in the Lord,
rejoice in Jehovah,
rejoice in the Lord,
and rejoice in Your Holy Name.

Chorus:
I need You, every step,
all along the way,
I look to You, my God,
for You are forever the same.
and do not change.

Chorus:
I need You, every step,
all along the way,
I look to You, my God,
for You are forever the same.
and do not change.

Verse:
Blessed be the Lord,
blessed be Jehovah,
blessed be the Lord,
blessed be Your Holy Name.

Chorus:
I need You, every step,
all along the way,
I look to You, my God,
for You are forever the same.
and do not change.

62. Sing It Loud

Verse:
Praise Your holy name, praise Your holy name,
praise Your holy name God Almighty.
Praise Your holy name, praise
Your holy name,
praise Your holy name Abba Father.

Verse:
We worship Your holy name, we
worship Your holy name,
we worship Your holy name God Almighty.
We worship Your holy name, we
worship Your holy name,
we worship Your holy name Abba Father.

Chorus:
Sing it loud, sing it proud,
sing it over and over, and over again,
God is God and there is no other,
God is God and He does not change, He
is the same today, yesterday, and forever.

Verse:
Magnify Your holy name,
magnify Your holy name,
magnify Your holy name God Almighty.
Magnify Your holy name,
magnify Your holy name,
magnify Your holy name Abba Father.

Verse:
Blessed be Your holy name,
blessed be Your holy name,
blessed be Your holy name God Almighty.
Bless be Your holy name, blessed
be Your holy name,
blessed be Your holy name Abba Father.

Chorus:
Sing it loud, sing it proud,
sing it over and over, and over again,
God is God and there is no other,
God is God and He does not change, He
is the same today, yesterday, and forever.

Bridge:
Sing It Loud Sing It Proud.
Over and over, and over again.
God Is Always the same,
and there is no other.

Chorus:
Sing it loud, sing it proud,
sing it over and over, and over again,
God is God and there is no other,
God is God and He does not change, He
is the same today, yesterday, and forever.

Chorus:
Sing it loud, sing it proud,
sing it over and over, and over again,
God is God and there is no other,
God is God and He does not change, He
is the same today, yesterday, and forever.

63. His Great Love

Verse:
Seven little words,
that mean so very much,
God is love, and He loves you,
la - la - la, la - la - la - la.

Verse:
Yes, sing them out loud,
knowing it is so true,
God is love, and He loves me to.
la - la - la, la - la - la - la.

Chorus:
Hug it to your heart,
hold it in your hand,
the precious word of God,
that tells of His great love,
towards all men.

Verse:
With a joy filled heart,
tell it to your neighbor,
God is love, and He loves you,
la - la - la, la - la - la - la.

Chorus:
Hug it to your heart,
hold it in your hand,
the precious word of God,
that tells of His great love,
towards all men.

Bridge:
No matter what you've done,
no matter what you do,
God is love,
and He loves you too.

Chorus:
Hug it to your heart,
hold it in your hand,
the precious word of God,
that tells of His great love,
towards all men.

64. He Has Overthrown All

Verse:
Victory is mine, victory is mine,
God has gone before me,
and victory is mine.
Victory is mine, victory is mine,
God has gone before me,
and victory is mine.

Chorus:
He has overthrown all, the
pharoses in my life,
He has overthrown all,
bondage, sickness and lack, in my life,
and I will never see them again.

Verse:
Healing is mine, healing is mine,
by Jesus' stripes I am healed,
and healing is mine.
Healing is mine, healing is mine,
by Jesus' stripes I am healed,
and healing is mine,

Chorus:
He has overthrown all, the
pharoses in my life,
He has overthrown all,
bondage, sickness and lack, in my life,
and I will never see them again.

Verse:
Freedom is mine, freedom is mine,
God supplies all my needs,
and freedom is mine.
Freedom is mine, freedom is mine,
God supplies all my needs,
and freedom is mine.

Chorus:
He has overthrown all, the
pharoses in my life,
He has overthrown all,
bondage, sickness and lack, in my life,
and I will never see them again.

65. Step Up, Step Up

Verse:
Step up, step up, step up to the plate,
step up, step up, and get on first base.
Step up, step up, step up to the mark,
step up, step up, join and be a part .

Chorus:
What more is needed,
why hesitate,
all hands and hearts are needed,
so step up and do not wait.

Verse:
Step up, step up, step up to the line,
Step up, step up and cling to the Vine.
Step up, step up, step up to the tee,
Step up, step up over the
sand traps victoriously!

Chorus:
What more is needed,
why hesitate,
all hands and hearts are needed,
so step up and do not wait.

Bridge:
No time to wait, no time to hesitate,
so step up, pitch in,
and just do it.

Chorus:
What more is needed,
why hesitate,
all hands and hearts are needed,
so step up and do not wait.

Chorus:
What more is needed,
why hesitate,
all hands and hearts are needed,
so step up and do not wait.

66. You a Lone Are Worthy

Verse:
We shall joy in Your strength O Lord,
and greatly rejoice in salvation,
we are exceedingly glad,
with the joy of Your presence,
for we trust and rely in You.

Verse:
we place confidence in You Lord,
Your mercy and grace follow us daily,
we love You with a steadfast love,
and we will not be moved,
we will sing of and praise Your power.

Chorus:
Be exalted our most high God,
be exalted our Heavenly Father,
we lift You high O mighty God,
and praise Your Holy name.

Verse:
Teach us to hate all that You hate,
Your enemies are our enemies,
Your hand shall find Your enemies,
Your right hand all those hating You,
the Lord will swallow them
up in His wrath.

Chorus:
Be exalted our most high God,
be exalted our Heavenly Father,
we lift You high O mighty God,
and praise Your Holy name.

Bridge:
Give Him glory, give Him honor,
give Him praise, for He alone is worthy.

Chorus:
Be exalted our most high God,
be exalted our Heavenly Father,
we lift You high O mighty God,
and praise Your Holy name.

Bridge:
We give You glory, we give you honor,
we give You praise, for You
alone are worthy O' God.

Chorus:
Be exalted our most high God,
be exalted our Heavenly Father,
we lift You high O mighty God,
and praise Your Holy name.

67. Joyous Crazy Praise

Verse:
I lift my hands and my face,
I give You all my praise,
I worship You with all my heart,
my Lord, my King, my Everything.

Chorus:
I surrender all to You, my
heart, my body, my mind,
I surrender all to You, in
joyous crazy praise.

Verse:
I lift my voice and my ways,
in honest wholly praise,
draw me close and never let me go,
my Saviour, and my Redeemer.

Chorus:
I surrender all to You, my
heart, my body, my mind,
I surrender all to You, in
joyous crazy praise.

Bridge:
I praise You Lord Jesus,
with genuine Wholly praise,
and heart felt crazy praise,
all unto You,
who is my All in All and Everything.

Chorus:
I surrender all to You, my
heart, my body, my mind,
I surrender all to You, in
joyous crazy praise.

Verse:
I lift my heels and my heart,
in reverential praise,
I worship You come what may,
my Elder Brother, and my friend.

Chorus:
I surrender all to You, my
heart, my body, my mind,
I surrender all to You, in
joyous crazy praise.

Bridge 2:
I leap, I dance, I spin about,
I jump, I run, I shout real loud,
all in crazy praise of You Lord Jesus.

Chorus:
I surrender all to You, my
heart, my body, my mind,
I surrender all to You, in
joyous crazy praise.

Section Five

Prayerful Song Lyrics

68. Help Me Lord

Verse:
I am standing at the crossroads,
of this dark and lonely road,
looking for a sign, to know which
way, which way to go.

Chorus:
Lord, seeking and searching
while stumbling along my way,
what is my direction,
do I go or stay,
somewhere somehow,
I have lost my way,
help me Lord God, I pray.

Verse:
I am sitting reading God's word,
searching for hope and true life,
decisions all about, wanting to
make, make truly right.

Chorus:
Lord, seeking and searching
while stumbling along my way,
what is my direction,
do I go or stay,
somewhere somehow,
I have lost my way,
help me Lord God, I pray.

Bridge:
Lord, I honestly and truly do love You,
who are so very faithful and true,
my heart cries Lord, show me what to do,
even now I know that all my hope is in You.

Chorus:
Lord, seeking and searching
while stumbling along my way,
what is my direction,
do I go or stay,
somewhere somehow,
I have lost my way,
help me Lord God, I pray.

Verse:
Walking on a mountain top high,
following the narrow road,
snares along the way, taking
God's road step, after step .

Chorus:
Lord, seeking and searching
while stumbling along my way,
what is my direction,
do I go or stay,
somewhere somehow,
I have lost my way,
help me Lord God, I pray.

69. My Heart's Desire

Verse:
Help me be Your hands and feet,
help me show compassion.
Help me see and hear what
You see and hear,

Chorus:
For I want to be more like You,
my Lord, my Life, my Love.
I want to be more like You,
this is my heart's desire.

Bridge:
You are my everything,
and my all in all,
You are my whole life,
and my very breath.

Chorus:
For I want to be more like You,
my Lord, my Life, my Love.
I want to be more like You,
this is my heart's desire.

Verse:
Help me to be salt and light,
help me to walk Your word,
help me reach and touch who
You reach and touch.

Chorus:
For I want to be more like You,
my Lord, my Life, my Love.
I want to be more like You,
this is my heart's desire.

Verse:
Help me be Your hands and feet,
help me show compassion.
Help me see and hear what
You see and hear,

Chorus:
For I want to be more like You,
my Lord, my Life, my Love.
I want to be more like You,
this is my heart's desire.

70. Open The Eyes of My Heart

Verse:
His eye is as a flame of fire,
His eyes are looking to and fro,
His eye is on the sparrow,
in the heavenly or on the
Earth down below.

Verse:
His eye is guiding righteous men's steps,
His eyes are never closed in sleep,
His eye sees all, everywhere,
and from Him, not one thing
are we able to keep.

Chorus:
Open the eyes of my heart, to see and
understand Your will and Your ways,
Open the eyes of my heart, and let me see
them as You see them each and every day,
Open the eyes of my heart, and show me all
the tricks and traps that the enemy has laid,
Open the eyes of my heart, and
help me to never forget,
the price my Lord and Saviour,
for you and me has paid.

Verse:
His eye is as a flame of fire,
His eyes are looking to and fro,
His eye is on the sparrow,
in the heavenly or on the
Earth down below.

Chorus:
Open the eyes of my heart, to see and
understand Your will and Your ways,
Open the eyes of my heart, and let me see
them as You see them each and every day,
Open the eyes of my heart, and show me all
the tricks and traps that the enemy has laid,
Open the eyes of my heart, and
help me to never forget,
the price my Lord and Saviour,
for you and me has paid.

Verse:
His eye is guiding righteous men's steps,
His eyes are never closed in sleep,
His eye sees all, everywhere,
and from Him, not one thing
are we able to keep.

Chorus:
Open the eyes of my heart, to see and
understand Your will and Your ways,
Open the eyes of my heart, and let me see
them as You see them each and every day,
Open the eyes of my heart, and show me all
the tricks and traps that the enemy has laid,
Open the eyes of my heart, and
help me to never forget,
the price my Lord and Saviour,
for you and me has paid.

71. Set Us Free

Chorus:
He who the son sets free,
is free in deed.
Jesus has set me free,
at the cross in victory.
Choose life and be set free.

Verse:
Draw us close and set us free,
open eyes and hearts to see
that you are God
and Jesus Christ is Lord and King.

Verse:
Draw us close and set us free,
open eyes and hearts to see
that You are love,
and giver of eternity.

Chorus:
He who the son sets free,
is free in deed.
Jesus has set me free,
at the cross in victory.
Choose life and be set free.

Verse:
Draw us close and set us free,
open eyes and hearts to see
that You won't leave,
and that all truth is found in You.

Verse:
Draw us close and set us free,
open eyes and hearts to see
that You are God
and Jesus Christ is Lord and King.

Chorus:
He who the son sets free,
is free in deed.
Jesus has set me free,
at the cross in victory.
Choose life and be set free.

Chorus:
He who the son sets free,
is free in deed.
Jesus has set me free,
at the cross in victory.
Choose life and be set free.

72. The Only One

Verse:
Holy precious Son of God,
shine on me;
Precious Holy son, shine down on me,
You are the only one that I need,
Holy precious Son of God,
shine down on me.

Verse:
Precious Holy Ghost of God,
reign in me;
Precious Holy Ghost, reign all in me,
Jesus sent you down to live in me,
precious Holy Ghost of God,
reign all in me.

Chorus:
You are the only one I need,
and the only way,
You are the only one I need,
Praise Your holy name.

Verse:
Precious living word of God,
direct me ;
Precious living word of God, lead me,
from top to bottom, and deep within,
wash and purify me from all sin,
precious living word of God,
purify me.

Chorus:
You are the only one I need,
and the only way,
You are the only one I need,
Praise Your holy name.

Verse:
Holy precious Son of God,
shine on me;
Precious Holy son, shine down on me,
You are the only one that I need,
Holy precious Son of God,
shine down on me.

Chorus:
You are the only one I need,
and the only way,
You are the only one I need,
Praise Your holy name.

73. Great is Your Grace

Verse:
Walk with me hand-in-hand,
and face-to-face,
walk with me oh' My Lord,
great is your grace.

Chorus:
I'm in You and You're in me,
together we will stand victoriously,
oh' My Lord great is Your grace.

Verse:
Walk with me day and night,
through every trial.
walk with me light of lights,
great is Your grace.

Chorus:
I'm in You and You're in me,
together we will stand victoriously,
oh' My Lord great is Your grace.

Verse:
Walk with me heart-to-heart,
and name-to-name,
walk with me oh' My Lord.
great is Your grace.

Chorus:
I'm in You and You're in me,
together we will stand victoriously,
oh' My Lord great is Your grace.

Chorus:
I'm in You and You're in me,
together we will stand victoriously,
oh' My Lord great is Your grace.

74. In You Lord Jesus

Verse:
Hide me neath Your sheltering wing,
hold me in Your nail scared hand,
wash me in Your precious blood,
sing over me Your song of love.

Verse:
fill me with Your wondrous light,
Breathe in me Your breath of life,
feed me Your life giving bread,
direct my way Your way instead.

Chorus:
Hide me, hold me, never let me go,
wash me, feed me, direct me so I'll know,
my hope is in You, my life is in You,
my way is in You Lord Jesus.

Verse:
cradle me in Your peace, no harm,
Wrap me in Your loving arms,
mold me in Your will and way,
envelop me in Your embrace.

Chorus:
Hide me, hold me, never let me go,
wash me, feed me, direct me so I'll know,
my hope is in You, my life is in You,
my way is in You Lord Jesus.

Bridge:
I'm in You and You're in me,
together we stand victoriously,
washed in Your blood and
held in Your hand,
I will look to You in whose I am.

Chorus:
Hide me, hold me, never let me go,
wash me, feed me, direct me so I'll know,
my hope is in You, my life is in You,
my way is in You Lord Jesus.

Chorus:
Hide me, hold me, never let me go,
wash me, feed me, direct me so I'll know,
my hope is in You, my life is in You,
my way is in You Lord Jesus.

75. You Amaze Me

Verse:
Amaze me,
I stand amazed,
my awesome,
Almighty God.

Verse:
Free me,
I stand freed,
my awesome,
Almighty God.

Chorus:
You amaze me,
with Your mercy,
and love, and life,
now I'm able
to stand on the Rock,
steadfast in Christ Jesus.

Verse:
Search me,
I stand searched,
my awesome,
Almighty God.

Verse:
Cleanse me,
I stand cleansed,
my awesome,
Almighty God.

Chorus:
You amaze me,
with Your mercy,
and love, and life,
now I'm able
to stand on the Rock,
steadfast in Christ Jesus.

Bridge:
I am amazed, and astounded,
what You've done, and what You're doing,
is more than what I have,
asked, hoped for or even dreamed.

Chorus:
You amaze me,
with Your mercy,
and love, and life,
now I'm able
to stand on the Rock,
steadfast in Christ Jesus.

76. Light Of The World

Verse:
Light of the world, let Your
light shine over me,
expose the dark with Your marvelous light,
Light of the world, light my world,
that I walk in Your pure light.

Chorus:
Jesus, You are the Light of the world,
You are the Bright and Morning Star,
Your word is a lamp unto my feet,
and a light unto my pathway.

Verse:
Light of the world, fully shine
Your light through me,
reveal all of the hidden darkness,
Light of the world, light my world,
that I see the path to walk.

Chorus:
Jesus, You are the Light of the world,
You are the Bright and Morning Star,
Your word is a lamp unto my feet,
and a light unto my pathway.

Bridge:
Light my world,
light my path,
expose the dark,
reveal the light,
make it known,
shine forth Your marvelous light.

Chorus:
Jesus, You are the Light of the world,
You are the Bright and Morning Star,
Your word is a lamp unto my feet,
and a light unto my pathway.

Chorus:
Jesus, You are the Light of the world,
You are the Bright and Morning Star,
Your word is a lamp unto my feet,
and a light unto my pathway.

77. O Breath Of Life

Verse:
Breathe in us, breathe through us,
our breath is in You,
and we have none without You.

Verse:
In You we live and move,
and have our being,
for we are also Your offspring.

Chorus:
Breathe on us O Breath of Life,
and resurrect the dead places,
breathe in us O Breath of Life,
ignite the spark into a flame,
breathe through us O Breath of Life,
so we are being filled with
Your love and life.

Verse:
Breathe on us that we live,
Life flowing through our beings,
Your breath's the Spirit of life.

Chorus:
Breathe on us O Breath of Life,
and resurrect the dead places,
breathe in us O Breath of Life,
ignite the spark into a flame,
breathe through us O Breath of Life,
so we are being filled with
Your love and life.

Bridge:
On us, in us, through us,
we look to You, our everything.

Chorus:
Breathe on us O Breath of Life,
and resurrect the dead places,
breathe in us O Breath of Life,
ignite the spark into a flame,
breathe through us O Breath of Life,
so we are being filled with
Your love and life.

Tag:
Holy Breath,
Sweet Sweet Breath,
Life Giving Breath,
that sustains Us.
Holy Breath,
Sweet Sweet Breath,
Life Giving Breath,
That Sustains Us.

78. Breathe

Verse:
Breathe, Breathe, Breathe, Over
us Lord God Almighty.
Breathe, Breathe, Breathe,
Over us Almighty God.

Chorus:
Here we are,
To Honor You,
To Worship You,
To Await Your Holy Presence,
So we humbly ask,

Verse:
Breathe, Breathe, Breathe, Around
us Lord God Almighty.
Breathe, Breathe, Breathe,
Around us Almighty God.

Chorus:
Here we are,
To Honor You,
To Worship You,
To Await Your Holy Presence,
So we humbly ask,

Verse:
Breathe, Breathe, Breathe, In
us Lord God Almighty,
Breathe, Breathe, Breathe,
In us Almighty God.

Chorus:
Here we are,
To Honor You,
To Worship You,
To Await Your Holy Presence,
So we humbly ask,

Bridge:
Breathe over us,
Breathe around us,
Breathe in us,
Our Almighty God.

Chorus:
Here we are,
To Honor You,
To Worship You,
To Await Your Holy Presence,
So we humbly ask,

Section Six

Song LYRICS For Certain Times Of The Year

79. T'was Such a Hushed and Holy Night

Verse:
T'was such a hushed and Holy night,
that befell upon the whole earth,
the night Christ Jesus was born.

Verse:
T'was such a hushed and Glorious night,
that befell the whole entire earth,
the night God's Son was born.

Chorus:
Angels appeared in a Heavenly Host,
to shepherds in the field,
watching o'er their flocks of sheep,
on that awesome, awesome night.

Verse:
T'was such a victorious night,
that befell the whole entire earth,
the night God, in love, sent Christ.

Chorus:
Angels appeared in a Heavenly Host,
to shepherds in the field,
watching o'er their flocks of sheep,
on that awesome, awesome night.

Verse:
T'was such a hushed and Holy night,
that befell the whole entire earth,
bringing us back to our God.

Bridge:
Glory to God in the highest, we
bring great tidings of joy,
with peace and goodwill towards all men,
this night God's Son, Christ Jesus is born.

Chorus:
Angels appeared in a Heavenly Host,
to shepherds in the field,
watching o'er their flocks of sheep,
on that awesome, awesome night.

Verse:
T'was such a hushed and Holy night,
that befell upon the whole earth,
the night Christ Jesus was born.

Chorus:
Angels appeared in a Heavenly Host,
to shepherds in the field,
watching o'er their flocks of sheep,
on that awesome, awesome night,
on that Hushed and Holy Night.

80. Happy Birthday Jesus

Happy Birthday Jesus, Rejoice
and praise His Holy name.
Happy Birthday Jesus, He
is forever the same.
Happy Birthday Jesus, He loves
us with a love so strong.
Happy Birthday Jesus, He came
to earth making right wrongs.

Happy Birthday Jesus, He lived
and died and Lives again.
Happy Birthday Jesus, He won
over Hell and men's sin .
Happy Birthday Jesus, in Him
love, joy, and peace are true.
Happy Birthday Jesus, choose life
in Him, be complete, too.

81. *What Christmas is to Me*

Verse:
Not a bell, nor a tree, is what
Christmas is to me.
Not a present, nor a song, brings
me joy all year long.
Not a reef, nor candle light, gives
me such a Holy Night.
Not a turkey, nor a pie, upon
this choice do I rely.

Chorus:
My wish for you is to have a
Merry Christmas, for now and
all throughout the year.
Yes my wish for you is to have a
very Merry Christmas, for now and
all throughout the whole year.

Bridge:
It is all about Christ Jesus.
For God, so loved that He gave,
His only begotten Son.
To be the bridge between God and man,
In birth and death and resurrected glory.
Redeeming us from sin,
back to Father God.
So rejoice for the gift He has given
that will last for all eternity.

Chorus:
My wish for you is to have a
Merry Christmas, for now and
all throughout the year.
Yes my wish for you is to have a
very Merry Christmas, for now and
all throughout the whole year.

Verse:
Not a bell, nor a tree, is what
Christmas is to me.
Not a present, nor a song, brings
me joy all year long.
Not a reef, nor candle light, gives
me such a Holy Night.
Not a turkey, nor a pie, upon
this choice do I rely.

Chorus:
My wish for you is to have a
Merry Christmas, for now and
all throughout the year.
Yes my wish for you is to have a
very Merry Christmas, for now and
all throughout the whole year.

82. God's Gift

Verse:
He was not found under a Christmas tree,
He dwells in the hearts of you and me,
Whom choose Him and are set free,
Calling them out of darkness and death
into true light and life Eternally.

Chorus:
This gift God sent from Heaven above,
Called us back unto Himself,
proving His abundant Love,
Even though Adams choice
separated us from Him,
He sent His Son
who took our place
becoming our sin.

Verse:
The greatest gift I have ever received,
Was not found under a Christmas Tree,
But hung on a cross for me,
After 3 days He rose from the tomb,
in VICTORY, and life
flowing through Him.

Chorus:
This gift God sent from Heaven above,
Called us back unto Himself,
proving His abundant Love,
Even though Adams choice
separated us from Him,
He sent His Son
who took our place
becoming our sin.

Bridge:
So Jesus is the reason for the season
and all throughout the year,
God wants to make you His own again
by calling you to draw near,
accept God's Gift and receive His Love,
To Him you are so very dear,
do not fear, and be of good cheer,
call on Jesus He is right here.

Chorus:
This gift God sent from Heaven above,
Called us back unto Himself,
proving His abundant Love,
Even though Adams choice
separated us from Him,
He sent His Son
who took our place
becoming our sin.

83. Star So Big, Star So Bright

Verse:
O' what a wonder,
O' what a joy,
For sweet Jesus, Mary's baby boy
was born in a stable,
wrapped in swaddling clothes,
With a manger for His bed.

Chorus:
Star so big,
star so bright,
Hanging high up in the sky,
pointing down to the place
where He was laid.

Verse:
O' what a wonder,
O' what a joy,
Angels appear giving a message
to shepherds in a field,
of, peace on earth to men,
this night was born the Saviour.

Chorus:
Star so big,
star so bright,
Hanging high up in the sky,
pointing down to the place
where He was laid.

Verse:
O' what a wonder,
O' what a joy,
In wishing you a Merry Christmas,
because of what God did,
through His Son, Lord Jesus Christ,

Chorus:
Star so big,
star so bright,
Hanging high up in the sky,
pointing down to the place
where He was laid.

Chorus:
Star so big,
star so bright,
Hanging high up in the sky,
pointing down to the place
where He was laid.

84. Paid In Full

Verse:
The loveliest rose that I have ever seen,
is a blood red rose that reminded me,
of the blood that was shed, while He was
nailed to the tree, innocent of all sin.

Verse:
For this they nailed Him to
that old cruel tree.
Drop by drop His precious blood was shed,
washing away my sins, All that kept us away
from God, was placed upon Him then.

Bridge:
His only crime was His love for man,
and following His Father's plan.

Chorus:
Who was He, who was nailed to the tree?
He was the Lamb of God who did no sin,
wrongfully accused and His
Fathers only begotten son.
The lion of Judah who sits upon His throne,
Emanuel whose love He did show.
The Messiah whose battle was
not with man, but the prince
of darkness of this land.

Verse:
Then before dark, they took
Him off the tree,
when Jesus's life had fled away.
They placed Him in a tomb, until on
the third day, the rock was rolled away.

Verse:
Now the rock at the tomb
has been rolled away,
and God said, "come forth my beloved
son with God's Glory flowing through
Him, now sitting at God's right hand.

Chorus:
Who was He, who was nailed to the tree?
He was the Lamb of God who did no sin,
wrongfully accused and His
Fathers only begotten son.
The lion of Judah who sits upon His throne,
Emanuel whose love He did show.
The Messiah whose battle was
not with man, but the prince
of darkness of this land.

Verse:
Jesus, He won the battle over death,
and He is the victorious one, Yes, the debt
has been paid, for all who come unto Him.

Chorus:
Who was He, who was nailed to the tree?
He was the Lamb of God who did no sin,
wrongfully accused and His
Fathers only begotten son.
The lion of Judah who sits upon His throne,
Emanuel whose love He did show.
The Messiah whose battle was
not with man, but the prince
of darkness of this land.

85. Outside The City Gates

Verse:
Going outside the city gates,
and looking upon that hill,
there were three crosses in a row,
and all of them were filled.
The first and third men on their
cross, were worthy of their death,
but the man on the middle cross
was different from the rest.
The man who hung upon the second cross,
was innocent of all He bore.
They cruelly nailed His hands
and feet, and did a lot more.

Chorus:
They scourged Him, mocked Him,
plucked out His beard
and stripped Him,
and did a lot more.

Bridge:
He was the precious lamb of God,
whose blood was shed for you and me,
He was the precious lamb of God,
whose blood washed away our sins,
setting all men who believe free.

Chorus.
They scourged Him, mocked Him,
plucked out His beard
and stripped Him,
and did a lot more.

Verse:
Going outside the city gates and
looking upon that hill,
there were three crosses in a row,
and all of them were filled.
the first and third cross on that hill,
hung men guilty of all done,
but on that second cross hung
God's only begotten Son,
who paid the debt for all of man.
When He said "IT IS FINISHED,"
in Him we all won, in death
from sin, Victoriously.

Chorus.
They scourged Him, mocked Him,
plucked out His beard
and stripped Him,
and did a lot more.

Chorus.
They scourged Him, mocked Him,
plucked out His beard
and stripped Him,
and did a lot more.

86. God's Love

Verse:
God's love sent His Son to earth,
God's love made the way,
God's love kept Him upon that cross,
until the penalty
for us He did pay.

Chorus:
God's love put Him in that tomb,
God's love brought Him forth again,
and God's love gave us another
chance to come close to Him.

Verse:
God's love brought us from death to life.
God's love shed forth light,
God's love brought us out of darkness,
and brought us back to Him,
through His Son Jesus.

Chorus:
God's love put Him in that tomb,
God's love brought Him forth again,
and God's love gave us another
chance to come close to Him.

Bridge:
There is no love without God's love,
there is no love without Him,
there is no love without God's love,
open your heart and welcome Him in.

Chorus:
God's love put Him in that tomb,
God's love brought Him forth again,
and God's love gave us another
chance to come close to Him.

Chorus:
God's love put Him in that tomb,
God's love brought Him forth again,
and God's love gave us another
chance to come close to Him.

87. No Longer There

Verse:
Look upon the place where
He had been laid,
behold He is not there, He is risen,
Jesus Christ is no longer there in the tomb,
no longer in that place among the dead.

Verse:
Despised, rejected, and forsaken by men,
a man of sorrows and pains,
grief and sickness,
He was despised, like one from
whom men hide their faces,
and we did not appreciate His worth.

Chorus:
Yes, fear not, He is no longer there,
in the tomb, but He is risen,
no longer dead, but very much alive,
yes, be not afraid,
He is no longer there,
for Jesus Christ, is alive,
rejoice and praise His holy name.

Verse:
He was considered to be stricken by God,
truly smitten by Him and afflicted,
Jesus was cut off from the land of the living,
having become sin for all mankind.

Chorus:
Yes, fear not, He is no longer there,
in the tomb, but He is risen,
no longer dead, but very much alive,
yes, be not afraid,
He is no longer there,
for Jesus Christ, is alive,
rejoice and praise His holy name.

Bridge:
He was wounded for our transgressions,
and He was bruised for our iniquity,
the chastisement of our
peace was upon Him,
and by His stripes we are healed.

Chorus:
Yes, fear not, He is no longer there,
in the tomb, but He is risen,
no longer dead, but very much alive,
yes, be not afraid,
He is no longer there,
for Jesus Christ, is alive,
rejoice and praise His holy name.

88. *Thank You For The Blood*

Chorus:
Thank You for the blood, of Jesus,
thank You for our being
washed, and cleansed,
thank You for the blood, of Jesus,
thank You for our being made
whole, and free in Him.

Verse:
Are you washed in the blood of The Lamb,
are you washed in the blood of The Lamb,
Are you chosen by God, are
you cleansed and set free,
Are you washed in the blood of The Lamb.

Verse:
There is power in the blood of The Lamb,
there is power in the blood of The Lamb,
Are you chosen by God, are
you cleansed and set free,
There is power in the blood of The Lamb.

Chorus:
Thank You for the blood, of Jesus,
thank You for our being
washed, and cleansed,
thank You for the blood, of Jesus,
thank You for our being made
whole, and free in Him.

Verse:
We are washed in the blood of The Lamb,
We are washed in the blood of The Lamb,
We are chosen by God, We
are cleansed and set free,
We are washed in the blood of The Lamb.

Verse:
Thank You for the blood of The Lamb,
thank You for the blood of The Lamb,
We are chosen by God, we are
cleansed and set free,
We Thank You God, for the
blood of The Lamb.

Chorus:
Thank You for the blood, of Jesus,
thank You for our being
washed, and cleansed,
thank You for the blood, of Jesus,
thank You for our being made
whole, and free in Him.

Chorus:
Thank You for the blood, of Jesus,
thank You for our being
washed, and cleansed,
thank You for the blood, of Jesus,
thank You for our being made
whole, and free in Him.

Chorus:
Thank You for the blood, of Jesus,
thank You for our being
washed, and cleansed,
thank You for the blood, of Jesus,
thank You for our being made
whole, and free in Him.

Section Seven

Song Lyrics Based On God's Holy Word

89. Mighty To Deliver

Verse:
Gracious and merciful is Jehovah our God,
mighty in power to deliver,
His loving kindness it does surround,
hiding us in the shadow of His wings.
Hiding us in the shadow of His wings.

Verse:
Holy and righteous is Jehovah our God,
mighty in power to deliver,
Abba Father, creator of all,
the one and only true living God.
The one and only true and living God.

Chorus:
Yes, He is mighty to deliver,
making ways where there are no ways,
yes He is mighty to deliver,
and I will praise Him all of my days.
And I will praise Him all of my days.

Verse:
Gracious and wonderful is
Jehovah our God,
mighty in power to deliver,
He is speaking with a still small voice,
slow to anger in kindness and in truth.
Slow to anger in kindness and in truth.

chorus:
Yes, He is mighty to deliver,
making ways where there are no ways,
yes He is mighty to deliver,
and I will praise Him all of my days.
And I will praise Him all of my days.

Bridge:
He is perfect in all His ways,
God of the heavens,
holding us in the palm of His hand,
the God of the universe.
God of the universe,
God of the universe.
God of the universe.

chorus:
Yes, He is mighty to deliver,
making ways where there are no ways,
yes He is mighty to deliver,
and I will praise Him all of my days.
And I will praise Him all of my days.

90. Come in with Singing

Verse:
Whosoever goeth on and weepeth,
bearing, the basket of seed,
surely cometh in with singing,
bearing his sheaves, before him.

Verse:
I sing unto Jehovah a new song,
lift up your voices in praise,
make a joyful noise for the Lord,
and keep blessing His Name.

Chorus:
Jehovah is righteous,
He cuts asunder the cords of the wicked,
sing ye to Jehovah,
praise Him for He has delivered
the soul of the needy,
from the evil doer.

Bridge:
Sing ye to Him,
give praise to Him,
meditate on all His wonders.
enter His gates with thanksgiving,
and His courts with praise.

Chorus:
Jehovah is righteous,
He cuts asunder the cords of the wicked,
sing ye to Jehovah,
praise Him for He has delivered
the soul of the needy,
from the evil doer.

Verse:
O' sing O heavens and rejoice O' earth,
and break forth mountains with song,
for His people are comforted,
afflicted ones He pities.

Verse:
Whosoever goeth on and weepeth,
bearing, the basket of seed,
surely cometh in with singing,
bearing, his sheaves, before him,
bearing, his sheaves before him.

Chorus:
Jehovah is righteous,
He cuts asunder the cords of the wicked,
sing ye to Jehovah,
praise Him for He has delivered
the soul of the needy,
from the evil doer.

91. He Is

Verse:
He is the mighty great I Am;
the Prince of Peace indeed,
the Sacrificial Lamb of God,
who shed His blood for thee.

Chorus:
He loves us with a love so strong;
He is our love divine,
He died and rose the third day,
He is our God's true vine.

Verse:
He's the fairest of ten-thousands;
The bright and morning star,
the Lord of lords and King of kings,
who's hands and feet are scared.

Chorus:
He loves us with a love so strong;
He is our love divine,
He died and rose the third day,
He is our God's true vine.

Bridge:
He is closer than a brother,
and truer than a true friend,
He is the Truth, the light, and the Way,
purchasing us with His life.
and the shedding of His precious blood
while hanging on that wooden cross.

Chorus:
He loves us with a love so strong;
He is our love divine,
He died and rose the third day,
He is our God's true vine.

Chorus:
He loves us with a love so strong;
He is our love divine,
He died and rose the third day,
He is our God's true vine.

92. Seek Jehovah

Verse:
Seek ye Jehovah and His strength,
seek His face continually.
seek Jehovah, with all your might,
and rejoice in His Holy Name,
for he who seeks Him shall find
Him as God's word says.

Chorus:
Thy words have been found, and I eat them,
and Your word is to me for a joy
and a rejoicing of my heart,
for I have sought You, and found You.

Verse:
Give ye thanks to our Jehovah,
call to Jesus, in His name,
make Him known among people .
Boast yourselves, in His holy name,
and the heart of those seeking
Jehovah, rejoice.

Chorus:
Thy words have been found, and I eat them,
and Your word is to me for a joy
and a rejoicing of my heart,
for I have sought You, and found You.

Bridge:
Know that Jehovah, He is God,
He made us and we are His,
we are His people, and the
flock of His pasture.
chosen Sons of God are we.

Chorus:
Thy words have been found, and I eat them,
and Your word is to me for a joy
and a rejoicing of my heart,
for I have sought You, and found You.

Verse:
Seek ye Jehovah and His strength,
seek His face continually.
seek Jehovah, with your might,
and rejoice in His Holy Name,
and break out with singing a
new song to our God.

Chorus:
Thy words have been found, and I eat them,
and Your word is to me for a joy
and a rejoicing of my heart,
for I have sought You, and found You.

93. The Shepherd

Verse:
The Shepherd left the ninety-nine
looking for one lost sheep.
The Shepherd left the ninety-nine
when He heard it cry, help me!

Chorus:
The Shepherd is Jesus Christ
the Son of God indeed.
The sacrificial Lamb of God that
shed His blood for you and me,
who died and rose the third day,
now lives in me you see.

Verse:
The sheep they know the master's voice,
He calls them one by one.
The sheep they know the master's voice,
from another they will run.

Chorus:
The Shepherd is Jesus Christ
the Son of God indeed.
The sacrificial Lamb of God that
shed His blood for you and me,
who died and rose the third day,
now lives in me you see.

Bridge:
He leads them to the sweet-sweet grass
and quiet flowing stream;
He is with them day and night
a guard from their enemies.

Chorus:
The Shepherd is Jesus Christ
the Son of God indeed.
The sacrificial Lamb of God that
shed His blood for you and me,
who died and rose the third day,
now lives in me you see.

Verse:
I was a sheep outside the fold;
the Shepherd left to find.
I was a sheep outside the fold,
and was always on His mind.

Chorus:
The Shepherd is Jesus Christ
the Son of God indeed.
The sacrificial Lamb of God that
shed His blood for you and me,
who died and rose the third day,
now lives in me you see.

94. Yes, The Rock Christ Jesus

Verse:
Build your house on a sure foundation,
Stable, solid, for ever more.
Build your house on a sure foundation,
on the Rock Christ Jesus alone.

Chorus:
The rains descended,
and the floods did come,
and the winds how they did blow,
And beat upon that house;
And it did not fall:
for it was built upon The Rock.

Bridge:
Built upon a Rock,
Yes, The Rock, Christ Jesus.
Built upon a Rock,
Yes, Jesus Christ our Lord.
Built upon a rock,
Yes, the Rock Christ Jesus.
Built upon a rock,
Yes, Jesus Christ our Lord.

Chorus:
The rains descended,
and the floods did come,
and the winds how they did blow,
And beat upon that house;
And it did not fall:
for it was built upon The Rock.

Verse:
Build your house on a sure foundation,
Unmoving, rock solid and sure.
Build your house on a sure foundation,
On the Rock Christ, for ever more.

Chorus:
The rains descended,
and the floods did come,
and the winds how they did blow,
And beat upon that house;
And it did not fall:
for it was built upon The Rock.

95. Lord and Saviour

Verse:
Who was it who fashioned this world
by His spoken word?
God Almighty, Lord and Saviour,
and the One who orders our steps.
Who made man from dust
and breathed the breath of life in him?
God Almighty, Lord and Saviour,
And the One who gives us strength.

Verse:
Who hung the sun, the moon, and stars
in the sky so high?
God Almighty, Lord and Saviour,
and the One who is the light.
Who was the Word who,
took on flesh, and dwelled among us?
God Almighty, Lord and Saviour,
and the One who leads us Home.

Chorus:
call Him Lord, and Saviour,
and Shepherd of the sheep,
He is The Great I Am, and
God's only Begotten Son,
The Lilies of The Valley, and The
Bright and Morning Star,
The Prince of Peace, and The Truth,
The Life, The Way and The Door.
and a whole lot more.

Verse:
Who is the One who lived and died,
and lives in us now?
God almighty, Lord and Saviour,
Who gives us strength and life in Him.
Who took on our sin,
who was innocent of all sin ?
God almighty, Lord and Saviour,
and did set us free, from death.

Chorus:
call Him Lord, and Saviour,
and Shepherd of the sheep,
He is The Great I Am, and
God's only Begotten Son,
The Lilies of The Valley, and The
Bright and Morning Star,
The Prince of Peace, and The Truth,
The Life, The Way and The Door.
and a whole lot more.

Chorus:
call Him Lord, and Saviour,
and Shepherd of the sheep,
He is The Great I Am, and
God's only Begotten Son,
The Lilies of The Valley, and The
Bright and Morning Star,
The Prince of Peace, and The Truth,
The Life, The Way and The Door.
and a whole lot more.

96. God Given Dreams

Verse:
If God is for us who can be against us,
What is impossible for man is not for God,
God makes ways where there
seems to be no way.

Bridge:
Having a night dream or day dream,
it doesn't really matter,
if God gives the dream walk in it.

Verse:
Man plans his way but God
orders all his steps,
the steps of a righteous man
are ordered by God,
God has gone before us in our future.

Chorus:
God given dreams are big,
God given dreams are huge,
far beyond
the desires of our hearts.
God given dreams are unlimited,
God given dreams are possible,
more than we can hope to imagine.

Verse:
If God is for us who can be against us,
What is impossible for man is not for God,
God makes ways where there
seems to be no way.

Chorus:
God given dreams are big,
God given dreams are huge,
far beyond
the desires of our hearts.
God given dreams are unlimited,
God given dreams are possible,
more than we can hope to imagine.

Bridge:
Dream big, bigger than one's self,
dream high, higher than the ordinary,
dream grand, grander than
the Grand Canyon.
Dream far, further than natural sight,
dream great, greater than
man's understanding,
dream large, larger than the deep blue sea.

Chorus:
God given dreams are big,
God given dreams are huge,
far beyond
the desires of our hearts.
God given dreams are unlimited,
God given dreams are possible,
more than we can hope to imagine.

97. God, Himself is Love

Verse:
Love is clean,
and love is pure.
Love is true,
from God is sure.

Chorus:
Love is what brought us back to Him.
Love is what set us free from sin.
Love is what gave us another chance.
Love is why I am here today,
and love is why I choose to stay,

Verse:
Love is kind,
and love is good.
Love is whole,
a gift, not took.

Chorus:
Love is what brought us back to Him.
Love is what set us free from sin.
Love is what gave us another chance.
Love is why I am here today,
and love is why I choose to stay,

Bridge:
God, Himself is Love,
and His love made a way.
His love is so strong,
His love is so great,
that He sent His Son,
In whom the debt was paid.

Chorus:
Love is what brought us back to Him.
Love is what set us free from sin.
Love is what gave us another chance.
Love is why I am here today,
and love is why I choose to stay,

Chorus:
Love is what brought us back to Him.
Love is what set us free from sin.
Love is what gave us another chance.
Love is why I am here today,
and love is why I choose to stay,

98. You, Our God

Verse:
You have told us, to put on
Honor and Beauty.
You have given us a garment of Praise.
You have clothed us with Your Kindness.
You have enfolded us in Your
Loving arms, and Grace.

Verse:
You are the Fortress, of which
we run into my Lord,
You are our shield, buckler, and our defense.
You are the Strong Tower,
in which we come,
You are shelter under which we
come as a Hiding Place.

Chorus:
We enter Your gates with thanksgiving,
We enter Your courts with praise.
We look to You, our God, in
which comes our help,
And reverence Your Holy Name.

Verse:
The storms come suddenly
they try to over throw,
The winds strongly blow,
they try to beat down,
The waves they try to weaken, But
on The Rock, we're found.

Chorus:
We enter Your gates with thanksgiving,
We enter Your courts with praise.
We look to You, our God, in
which comes our help,
And reverence Your Holy Name.

Bridge:
We are standing, we are standing,
we are standing, on the Rock Christ Jesus,
We are standing, we are standing,
we are standing, on the Rock shod dry.
We are standing, we are standing,
we are standing, on the Rock Christ Jesus,
We are standing, we are standing,
we are standing, on the Rock shod dry.

Chorus:
We enter Your gates with thanksgiving,
We enter Your courts with praise.
We look to You, our God, in
which comes our help,
And reverence Your Holy Name.

99. God The Sun

Verse:
With eyes like flames of fire,
a sword coming out of His mouth,
a golden girdle around His paps,
and feet as fine brass.
A countenance brighter than the sun,
with hair as white wool,
riding a white horse,
ruling with a rod of iron.

Verse:
He walks among the 7 lamp stands,
and holds the 7 stars in His hand,
in which He also broke the 7 seals,
and judges' man.
Who bares us about in His body
and holds us in His hand
who sits on the right hand of His Father,
and waits for the finished plan.

Chorus:
He, is the same, today,
yesterday, and forever,
the Alpha and omega, the First and the
Last and the beginning and the End.
He is the Lord of the harvest,
the Head of the Church,
the Great I Am,
and the Bridegroom waiting for His bride.

Verse:
With a voice that sounds like thunder,
and a whisper on the wind,
or many-many waters,
or a trumpet blast.
A roaring lion,
or a meek lamb,
a gentle dove,
or True God and True man

Bridge:
Jesus is The King of kings,
and Lord of lords,
He is The Prince of Peace indeed,
The Truth, The Light and The Door,

Chorus:
He, is the same, today,
yesterday, and forever,
the Alpha and omega, the First and the
Last and the beginning and the End.
He is the Lord of the harvest,
the Head of the Church,
the Great I Am,
and the Bridegroom waiting for His bride.

100. Nuggets Of Gold Revealed from The Psalms

Verse:
The heavens declare the glory of God,
and the firmaments show His handy work,
day unto day utters speech, and night
unto night reveals knowledge,
their light has gone through out
all the earth, and their words
to the end of the world,
in them He has set a tabernacle for
the sun, which is like the bride groom
coming out of his chamber,
and rejoiceth like a strong
man, to run his race.

Verse:
The law of the Lord is perfect
converting the soul,
the testimony of the Lord is sure
making wise the simple,
the statutes of the Lord are right rejoicing
the heart, the commandment of the Lord
is pure enlightening the eye, the fear
of the Lord is clean enduring forever
the judgments of the Lord are true,
and righteous all together.
More are they to be desired, are
they than gold, sweeter also than
the honey in the honey comb,

Chorus:
may the name of the God
of Jacob, defend you,
may He send His help out of the sanctuary,
and strengthen you out of Zion,
may the Lord fulfill all of your petitions.

Bridge:
oh' Lord, thou art my strength,
and my redeemer,
blessed be the rock, and let the God
of my salvation be exulted,

Verse:
The earth is the Lord's in all its fullness,
the world and all who dwell there within,
for He has founded it upon the seas,
and established it upon the waters,
the Lord of host, He is the King of
Glory Good and upright is the Lord,
therefore He teaches sinners in the way,
the humble He guides in justice,
and the humble He teaches His way.
All the paths of the Lord, are mercy
and truth, to such that keep His
covenants, and testimony,

Verse:
the secret of the Lord, is with
those who fear Him,
and He will show them His covenants.
The Lord is my light, and my salvation,
whom shall I fear,
the Lord is the strength of my life,
of whom shall I be afraid?
Show me thy ways, and teach
me your ways, oh' Lord,

Chorus:
may the name of the God
of Jacob, defend you,
may He send His help out of the sanctuary,
and strengthen you out of Zion,
may the Lord fulfill all of your petitions.

Chorus:
may the name of the God
of Jacob, defend you,
may He send His help out of the sanctuary,
and strengthen you out of Zion,
may the Lord fulfill all of your petitions.

Verse:
wait on the Lord and be of good courage,
and He shall strengthen our hearts,
the Lord is my strength and my shield
The Lord is the saving refuge
of the anointed,
the voice of the Lord is over the
waters, the God of Glory thunders,
the voice of the Lord, is powerful, the
voice of the Lord is full of majesty,
the Lord sat enthroned at the flood,
and the Lord sits as King forever.

101. Here From Heaven

Verse:
Sew to yourselves in righteousness,
reap in mercy, and break up
your fallow ground,
for it is time to seek the Lord, till He
come and rain righteousness upon you

Chorus:
If My people who are called by My name
will humble themselves and
pray and seek My face
and turn from their wicked ways,
then will I hear from heaven and will
forgive their sin and will heal their land.

Verse:
If you continue in your faith,
established and firm not moved from
the hope held out in the gospel,
this is the gospel that you heard,
proclaimed to every creature under heaven.

Chorus:
If My people who are called by My name
will humble themselves and
pray and seek My face
and turn from their wicked ways,
then will I hear from heaven and will
forgive their sin and will heal their land.

Bridge:
O' Lord God, of our fathers, are You
not the God, who is in Heaven,
You rule over all the kingdoms
of the nations,
power and might are in Your hands,
and no one can withstand You.

Chorus:
If My people who are called by My name
will humble themselves and
pray and seek My face
and turn from their wicked ways,
then will I hear from heaven and will
forgive their sin and will heal their land.

words found in: 2 Chr. 7:14, 2 Chr. 20:6,
Hosea 10:12, and Col. 1:23, (NIV)

102. God is good

Verse:
He has shown you, O' man, what is good,
and what does the Lord require of you,
but to do justly, to love mercy,
and to walk humbly with your God.

Verse:
Rejoice not over me, enemy,
when I fall, through God, I shall arise,
when I sit in darkness, I'm not afraid.
the Lord, shall be a light unto me.

Chorus:
Do not fear other gods,
nor bow yourselves to them,
nor serve them,
nor sacrifice to them.
But the Lord, who had brought
us up out of darkness,
being separated from God,
with strength and stretched out arm,
Him alone shall you fear,
and Him shall you worship,
and Him shall you sacrifice to.
Fear God alone, and He
shall deliver you out
of the hand of your enemies.

Bridge:
If God is for us,
who can be against us?
Choose ye this day,
whom you shall serve,
as for me and my household,
we shall serve the Lord.

Chorus:
Do not fear other gods,
nor bow yourselves to them,
nor serve them,
nor sacrifice to them.
But the Lord, who had brought
us up out of darkness,
being separated from God,
with strength and stretched out arm,
Him alone shall you fear,
and Him shall you worship,
and Him shall you sacrifice to.
Fear God alone, and He
shall deliver you out
of the hand of your enemies.

103. He is God

Chorus:
He is the Lord, our God,
and there is none else,
there is no god besides Him.
The earth is His,
and the fullness there of.

Verse:
God formed the light,
and created darkness.
God made the peace,
and created evil.
God formed the earth.
and created the heavens,

Verse:
God formed first man,
and created woman.
God made all good,
and created free choice.
God formed beauty,
and created all colors.

Chorus:
He is the Lord, our God,
and there is none else,
there is no god besides Him.
The earth is His,
and the fullness there of.

Bridge:
Look there unto God,
through His son,
who died for you and me,
accept Him as Lord, and God,
and be saved, All the ends of the earth,
for He is our Creator,
and there is none other.

Chorus:
He is the Lord, our God,
and there is none else,
there is no god besides Him.
The earth is His,
and the fullness there of.

104. Walk By Faith

Verse:
Walk by faith
and not by sight,
peace be still
all storms of the night.

Chorus:
Jesus is the Prince of Peace,
a lamp to light the path for our feet.
Jesus is the Son of God,
whose blood was shed for one and all.

Verse:
Walk by faith
and not by sight,
carry Christ's Cross
so high true and right.

Chorus:
Jesus is the Prince of Peace,
a lamp to light the path for our feet.
Jesus is the Son of God,
whose blood was shed for one and all.

Bridge:
For it's neither by might nor by power,
but by my Spirit sayeth the Lord.
So run the race set before you,
ask, seek and knock at the door,
Jesus Christ is the door and a lot more.

Chorus:
Jesus is the Prince of Peace,
a lamp to light the path for our feet.
Jesus is the Son of God,
whose blood was shed for one and all.

Verse:
Walk by faith
and not by sight,
firm shod dry,
on the Rock Christ.

Chorus:
Jesus is the Prince of Peace,
a lamp to light the path for our feet.
Jesus is the Son of God,
whose blood was shed for one and all.

105. Revealed

Verse:
For there is nothing hid, which
shall not be manifested.
neither was anything kept secret,
but that it should be revealed.

Chorus:
For there is nothing covered,
that shall not be revealed,
and hid that shall not be known.

Verse:
For what is hidden, is meant
to be fully disclosed.
And whatever is craftily concealed,
is to be brought to the open.

Chorus:
For there is nothing covered,
that shall not be revealed,
and hid that shall not be known.

Bridge:
Our work will be shown for what it is,
because the day will bring it to light,
it will be revealed with fire,
and the fire will test, the quality
of each man's work.

Chorus:
For there is nothing covered,
that shall not be revealed,
and hid that shall not be known.

106. Worthy

Verse:
Whosoever, shall confess Me before men,
him will I confess also before My Father
who is in heaven,

Chorus:
He that finds his life, shall loose it,
and he that loses his life for
My sake, shall find it.

Verse:
but whosoever shall deny Me before men,
him I shall deny also before My Father
who is in heaven.

Chorus:
He that finds his life, shall loose it,
and he that loses his life for
My sake, shall find it.

Bridge:
He that does not love father or mother
more than Me, is worthy of Me,
and he that does not love son or daughter
more than Me, is worthy of Me.
And he that takes up his cross, and
follow after Me, is worthy of Me.

Chorus:
He that finds his life, shall loose it,
and he that loses his life for
My sake, shall find it.

107. God's Solution

Verse:
By Jesus we also have access
by faith into this grace
wherein which we stand,
and rejoice in hope of the glory of God.

Chorus:
God so loved, He gave,
I so needed, I took,
Jesus Christ, God's gracious gift.

Verse:
God's solution was to give,
His only begotten Son,
I needed desperately,
so I took His precious gift,
that I could live in Him.

Chorus:
God so loved, He gave,
I so needed, I took,
Jesus Christ,
God's gracious gift.

Verse:
Christ Jesus, came and took my place,
becoming sin for me,
giving me a chance, to come back to God,
He came down born as man.

Chorus:
God so loved, He gave,
I so needed, I took,
Jesus Christ, God's gracious gift.

Bridge:
Jesus Christ, God's solution,
the one and only way,
back to the Father for me,
Father God did make.

Chorus:
God so loved, He gave,
I so needed, I took,
Jesus Christ, God's gracious gift.

108. God is Great

Verse:
How big is your God, the
one who created you?
How big have you allowed Him to be?
and how much power does He have?
Is He larger than life; is He
greater than great,
Is He the holiest of holy's?
and is He true to His word?

Chorus:
God is great, and greatly to be praised,
so we bow our heads and bend our knees,
and render unto God the
praise He should receive.

Verse:
Has He been put in a box;
only out when needed?
Have there been limits put on Him?
What is He allowed to do?
The Creator cannot be
ruled by the creation.
God is the Creator,
limitless. He is the one and only God.

Chorus:
God is great, and greatly to be praised,
so we bow our heads and bend our knees,
and render unto God the
praise He should receive.

Verse:
God is holy and righteous, pure,
just, true, and faithful,
He is gracious, merciful, and loving,
and God is always in control.
His ways and thoughts are higher
than our ways and thoughts,
He does not change for He is the same
and His throne's in the highest heaven.

Chorus:
God is great, and greatly to be praised,
so we bow our heads and bend our knees,
and render unto God the
praise He should receive.

Bridge:
The whole earth is His and
the fullness there of.
He hung the sun, moon and stars in the sky.
and He holds us in the palm of His hand.

Chorus:
God is great, and greatly to be praised,
so we bow our heads and bend our knees,
and render unto God the
praise He should receive.

109. Lift Him High

Verse:
Up rise worship and praises to God,
down fall the showers of blessing.
In comes God's marvelous light,
out goes the darkness.

Verse:
Over us is God's sheltering wing,
under our feet is the enemy.
Come Jesus said, follow Me,
go and sin no more.

Chorus:
Be not just a hearer,
but a doer of God's word,
honor Him indeed,
for He is worthy of all our praise,
and lift Him high,
yes, lift Him high in praise every day.

Verse:
Up rise worship and praises to God,
down fall the showers of blessing.
In comes God's marvelous light,
out goes the darkness.

Verse:
Over us is God's sheltering wing,
under our feet is the enemy.
Come Jesus said, follow Me,
go and sin no more.

Chorus:
Be not just a hearer,
but a doer of God's word,
honor Him indeed,
for He is worthy of all our praise,
and lift Him high,
yes, lift Him high in praise every day.

110. He is the Lord...

Verse:
He is the Lord our redeemer,
and He who formed us in our mother's
womb, is the Lord, who made all things.

Verse:
He is the Lord, who confirms His word,
and preforms the counsel of His
messengers, faithful in all His ways.

Chorus:
The One and only true living God,
is in us and among us, and He alone is God,
there is none other, no, there is none other.

Bridge:
From the rising of the sun, to
the setting of the sun,
God is God, and there is none other.

Chorus:
The One and only true living God,
is in us and among us, and He alone is God,
there is none other, no, there is none other.

Chorus:
The One and only true living God,
is in us and among us, and He alone is God,
there is none other, no, there is none other.

111. Many Members, One Body

Verse:
There are many members in the body
of Christ, all, so very important,
none of them being the same.

Verse:
Protect each member of the body as
precious, vitally needed to function,
in fulfilling God's plans.

Chorus:
For we are the body of Christ,
and members in particular,
not all an eye, nor a foot, but,
placed where God pleases.

Verse:
The church, the body with Christ Jesus
at the head, connected one to another,
many members, one body.

Chorus:
For we are the body of Christ,
and members in particular,
not all an eye, nor a foot, but,
placed where God pleases.

112. The People of God

Chorus:
In times past we were not a people,
but are now the people of God,
who had not obtained mercy,
but now have obtained mercy.

Verse:
We are a chosen generation,
a royal priesthood,
a holy nation unto God,
a peculiar people,
Christ suffered for us,
leaving us an example,
that we should show forth
the praises of Him,
who has called us out of darkness
into His marvelous light.

Verse:
Chosen by God and precious in His sight,
also as living stones,
are built up a Spiritual house,
a Holy priesthood
to offer up a Spiritual sacrifice,
acceptable to God by Jesus Christ,
the chief cornerstone, and we who
believe will not be confounded.

Chorus:
In times past we were not a people,
but are now the people of God,
who had not obtained mercy,
but now have obtained mercy.

Verse:
We were as sheep going astray, scattered,
but have now returned
to the Shepherd and Bishop of our soul,
who Himself bore our sins
in His own body, that we
being dead to sins,
should live unto righteousness in our God,
for by the stripes that Jesus Christ
bore for us we were healed.

Chorus:
In times past we were not a people,
but are now the people of God,
who had not obtained mercy,
but now have obtained mercy.

113. The Whole Body

Chorus:
If the whole body were an eye,
where would be the hearing.
If the whole body were the ear,
where would be the smelling.
The body has many members, if they were
one member, where would be the body.

Verse:
If the foot says, because I am not the hand,
is it not of the body.

Verse:
If the ear says, I am not the eye,
so I am not of the body.

Chorus:
If the whole body were an eye,
where would be the hearing.
If the whole body were the ear,
where would be the smelling.
The body has many members, if they were
one member, where would be the body.

Bridge:
The eye cannot say to the hand,
I have no need of you.
As the head cannot say to the
feet, I have no need of you,
God has set the members in the
body, as it has pleased Him.

Chorus:
If the whole body were an eye,
where would be the hearing.
If the whole body were the ear,
where would be the smelling.
The body has many members, if they were
one member, where would be the body.

114. One Body in Christ

Verse:
Will you offer yourself as, a living sacrifice,
holy acceptable unto God,
we should present our bodies to God,
which is our reasonable service.

Verse:
Prefer one another, be not
slothful in business,,
show kind affection one to another,
be fervent in spirit serving the
Lord, renew the mind with God's
word and be transformed.

Chorus:
One body in Christ, with many members,
set where God has placed us,
in the house of God.

Verse:
Show mercy with cheerfulness,
give with simplicity,
hate evil and cling to that which is good,
rejoice with them that do rejoice, and
weep with them that do also weep.

Chorus:
One body in Christ, with many members,
set where God has placed us,
in the house of God.

115. In These Times (Possible Rap)

Chorus:
God is calling, calling us out,
out from among them.
God is drawing, drawing us,
us back unto Himself.

Verse:
In these times, evil is called good,
and good is called evil.
the days are perilous, and of great stress.
troubles are hard to deal with,
and quite hard to bear.

Verse:
In these times, will be lovers of
self, and utterly self-centered.
they are lovers of money, aroused by greed .
people are full of pride,
contemptuous boasters.

Chorus:
God is calling, calling us out,
out from among them.
God is drawing, drawing us,
us back unto Himself.

Verse:
In these times, they are scoffers,
disobeying parents.
are those who are ungrateful,
as well as profane.
without human affection, and relentless .

Verse:
In these times, they will be false
accusers, who are also intemperate.
people loose in morals, haters of good.
they are treacherous betrayers,
inflated with self-conceit.

Chorus:
God is calling, calling us out,
out from among them.
God is drawing, drawing us,
us back unto Himself.

Verse:
In these times, are lovers of pleasures,
pursuing vein amusements.
into loving self, not loving God.
holding a form of piety,
denying their profession.

Chorus:
God is calling, calling us out,
out from among them.
God is drawing, drawing us,
us back unto Himself.
The scripture I used in the wording
of the verses is taken from, 2
Timothy 3:1-5. Amp Version.

116. God's Abiding Grace

Chorus:
God loved us with a love so strong,
He sent His only begotten Son,
to come down here and take our place,
and show us God's abiding grace.

Verse:
Love came down to earth as man,
Love only did His Fathers plan,
Jesus is our Love, Jesus is our Life,
So come unto Him who hung on high.

Verse:
Love hung Himself upon a tree,
Taking the place of you and me.
Jesus is our Love, Jesus is our Life,
So come unto Him who was lifted high.

Chorus:
God loved us with a love so strong,
He sent His only begotten Son,
to come down here and take our place,
and show us God's abiding grace.

Verse:
Love took our place dying for our sins,
Love rose again to bring us Life in Him.
Jesus is our Love, Jesus is our Life,
So come unto Him who sits on high.

Chorus:
God loved us with a love so strong,
He sent His only begotten Son,
to come down here and take our place,
and show us God's abiding grace.

Chorus:
God loved us with a love so strong,
He sent His only begotten Son,
to come down here and take our place,
and show us God's abiding grace.

117. The Cause

Chorus:
With the cause there is a cost,
well worth the price paid,
with the cause there is a choice
man's will or God's way.

Verse:
Look to God and take up His cause
Holding fast to what is right, In
the power of His might,
look to God and take on His cause
and hold tight with all your might,
keeping God's standard high.

Verse:
With God's cause we've already won,
for the battle is the Lord's,
with God's cause life is not lost,
when laid down for someone else.

Chorus:
With the cause there is a cost,
well worth the price paid,
with the cause there is a choice
man's will or God's way.

Verse:
Look to God and take up His cause
and walk in God's truth and light
look to God and take on His cause
and not slack but stand fast and fight.

Chorus:
With the cause there is a cost,
well worth the price paid,
with the cause there is a choice
man's will or God's way.

Bridge:
We've got the tools, the armor is ours,
so take up God's cause, and
fight, fight, fight.

Chorus:
With the cause there is a cost,
well worth the price paid,
with the cause there is a choice
man's will or God's way.

118. Not With Man

Chorus:
We are in a battle,
but not with flesh and blood,
we are in a battle,
but not with man.

Verse:
We are called to the battle line,
always marching forward,
with no retreat,
and no backing up in us.

Verse:
The enemy all around us,
but Jesus has our back,
He is our defense,
our shield and buckler.

Chorus:
We are in a battle,
but not with flesh and blood,
we are in a battle,
but not with man.

Verse:
Our battle is with the devil,
the enemy of our soul,
who hates us so,
for he truly hates God.

Chorus:
We are in a battle,
but not with flesh and blood,
we are in a battle,
but not with man.

Bridge:
The army of the Lord, marches out to war,
we take our stand, and hold our ground,
knowing in Christ we have already won.

Chorus:
We are in a battle,
but not with flesh and blood,
we are in a battle,
but not with man.

119. In Your Image

Verse:
I am made in Your image,
fashioned by Your loving hands,
we are made in Your image,
none alike, but all the same.

Verse:
I was made in Your image,
created to love You Lord,
we were made in Your image,
with all our days already planned.

Chorus:
In Your image,
Almighty God,
fearfully and wonderfully made,
we are made in Your image Abba Father.

Verse:
I am made in your image,
fashioned by your Almighty hands,
we are made in Your image,
from the very beginning.

Chorus:
In Your image,
Almighty God,
fearfully and wonderfully made,
we are made in Your image Abba Father.

Chorus:
In Your image,
Almighty God,
fearfully and wonderfully made,
we are made in Your image Abba Father.

120. I'm Calling You Out

Chorus:
I'm calling you out,
calling you out,
yes, calling you out from among them.

Verse:
My people come out of the midst of her,
and let every man save his life,
from the fierce anger of the lord.

Verse:
Let not destruction come upon you,
through her punishment for sin and guilt,
it is the time for the Lord's vengeance.

Chorus:
I'm calling you out,
calling you out,
yes, calling you out from among them.

Verse:
Babylon who dwells by many waters,
rich in many treasures your end has come,
and the line measuring your life is cut.

Chorus:
I'm calling you out,
calling you out,
yes, calling you out from among them.

Verse:
Great Babylon, she has fallen,
by God she has reaped what she has sown,
and she has fallen and been destroyed.

Bridge:
Come away from the sin,
come away from the lies,
come away from the destruction,
follow after Me,
and have eternal life.

Chorus:
I'm calling you out,
calling you out,
yes, calling you out from among them.

121. Keep your Eyes Upon Jesus

Chorus:
Keep your eyes upon Jesus,
keep your eyes upon Him,
neither look left nor right, nor run and hide,
but keep your eyes upon the Lord.

Verse:
The Lord will march out like a champion,
like a warrior, He will stir up His zeal,
with a shout He will raise the battle cry,
and will triumph over His enemies.

Verse:
The Lord is passionate about you,
and He is fighting, for His beloved people,
and destroying utterly their enemies,
that are strongholds against their
hope through great zeal.

Chorus:
Keep your eyes upon Jesus,
keep your eyes upon Him,
neither look left nor right, nor run and hide,
but keep your eyes upon the Lord.

Verse:
Just as the Father has loved Jesus,
He has loved us, so abide in His love,
for He is the True Vine on which we rely,
and the Father is the loving vinedresser.

Verse:
Jesus said this is My commandment,
to love each other, even as I have loved you,
the eye can't say to the hand
I don't need you,
for we do need each other so show love.

Bridge:
Look to Jesus,
from whence comes our help,
He is our everything,
and our all in all,
beautiful to behold.

Chorus:
Keep your eyes upon Jesus,
keep your eyes upon Him,
neither look left nor right, nor run and hide,
but keep your eyes upon the Lord.

Chorus:
Keep your eyes upon Jesus,
keep your eyes upon Him,
neither look left nor right, nor run and hide,
but keep your eyes upon the Lord.

122. Our God, our Creator

Verse:
The most high over all the earth,
holds us in His hands,
The Lord mighty in battle,
teaches our hands to war.
Creator of the ends of the earth,
formed us in our mother's womb,
Father of the fatherless,
will never leave us nor forsake us.

Chorus:
We acknowledge You our God,
we exalt You our Creator,
to You all glory, honor, and praise,
for the rest of our days.

Verse:
God that judgeth in the earth,
all His words and ways are true,
He is able to keep you from falling,
who strengthens feeble knees.
The Holy one in the midst of thee,
giving wisdom and strength,
the majesty in the Heavens,
watching o'er us day and night.

Chorus:
We acknowledge You our God,
we exalt You our Creator,
to You all glory, honor, and praise,
for the rest of our days.

Verse:
Thou that dwells between the Cherubim,
from whom nothing is hid,
the incorruptible God,
makes us in His image.
Who's ways are higher than our ways,
And thoughts higher than our thoughts,
Hides us neath the shadow of His wings,
Held cradled in God's loving hands.

Chorus:
We acknowledge You our God,
we exalt You our Creator,
to You all glory, honor, and praise,
for the rest of our days.

123. To God I Call

Verse:
Call on Me sayeth the Lord,
and I will show you things-
things that you know nothing about.

Verse:
My voice is unto Jehovah,
and He answers me-
answers me from His Holy Hill.

Chorus:
Yes, to God I call, and Jehovah saves me,
I call to God Most High,
give ear to my voice when I call.

Bridge 1:
To God, the Most High God,
I call, I call to Thee,
Saviour of my soul.

Verse:
In my calling answereth Thou me,
O God of my righteousness,
O God, favor me and hear my prayer.

Verse:
Unto thee O Jehovah,
I call my Rock-
my Rock, be not silent unto me.

Chorus:
Yes, to God I call, and Jehovah saves me,
I call to God Most High,
give ear to my voice when I call.

Bridge II:
I call to You my God,
I look to You,
I need You,
I love You my God,
my everything and all in all.

Chorus:
Yes, to God I call, and Jehovah saves me,
I call to God Most High,
give ear to my voice when I call.

Chorus:
Yes, to God I call, and Jehovah saves me,
I call to God Most High,
give ear to my voice when I call.

124. I Look To You My God

Verse:
Though I fall, I will arise,
Though things may appear
dark and unsure,
God is my light.

Chorus:
My anchor, my hope, I hold fast to You,
my everything, my all in all,
I look to You my God.

Bridge:
Hold fast and never let go,
through the storm and through the calm,
tie to Him, cling to Him, look to Him,
He is my everything, He is my all in all,
He is my God!

Chorus:
My anchor, my hope, I hold fast to You,
my everything, my all in all,
I look to You my God.

Verse:
Though I fall, I will arise,
Though things may appear
dark and unsure,
God will be my light.

Chorus:
My anchor, my hope, I hold fast to You,
my everything, my all in all,
I look to You my God.

Bridge:
Hold fast and never let go,
through the storm and through the calm,
tie to Him, cling to Him, look to Him,
He is my everything, He is my all in all,
He is my God!

Chorus:
My anchor, my hope, I hold fast to You,
my everything, my all in all,
I look to You my God.

125. God Says

Chorus:
God says seek Me and you shall find Me,
knock and the door will be opened to you,
He says if you draw close to Me,
I will draw close to you.

Verse:
I am the apple of God's eye,
I am precious in His sight,
I am His beloved,
and God I love, who first loved me.

Chorus:
God says seek Me and you shall find Me,
knock and the door will be opened to you,
He says if you draw close to Me,
I will draw close to you.

Verse:
I am abundantly blessed,
and I am a child of God,
held in the palm of His hand,
fearfully and wonderfully made.

Verse:
I am an heir of God and,
I am a joint heir with Jesus Christ,
and a king and priest,
called unto His royal priesthood.

Chorus:
God says seek Me and you shall find Me,
knock and the door will be opened to you,
He says if you draw close to Me,
I will draw close to you.

Bridge:
Seek Me,
and find Me,
draw close,
and never let go.

Chorus:
God says seek Me and you shall find Me,
knock and the door will be opened to you,
He says if you draw close to Me,
I will draw close to you.

126 Proclaim, Declare, and Decree

chorus:
It is written! and Thus says the Lord!
Say what God's word says,
Proclaim, Declare, and Decree!
Through Christ Jesus in victory.,

Verse:
By Jesus stripes I am healed,
that which I put my hands to prosper,
in my weakness I am made
strong in You God,
God turns what was meant for evil to good,
and makes ways when there
seems to be no way!

chorus:
It is written! and Thus says the Lord!
Say what God's word says,
Proclaim, Declare, and Decree,
Through Christ Jesus in victory.,

Verse:
I am the apple of God's eye,
His beloved, and precious in His sight,
a soldier in God's mighty army,
redeemed from the curse of the law,
God is the creator, and Jesus is Lord!

Bridge:
Proclaim it across the rooftops,
Declare it around the world,
and Decree it with God's holy Word,
choose life in God and live, through
His only begotten Son!
Our Lord and Savior JESUS CHRIST!

Chorus:
It is written! and Thus says the Lord!
Say what God's word says,
Proclaim, Declare, and Decree,
Through Lord Christ Jesus in victory.,

Tag:
Proclaim,
Declare, and Decree,
for it is written,
and thus says the Lord!

127. I Need You

Verse:
My eyes are upon You, my God,
my hope is in You, my Lord,
my life is through You, my
God, my Abba Father.

Chorus:
With every step I take,
and every breath I breathe,
both day and night,
I need You,
my Lord God.

Verse:
You are my hiding place, my God,
You are my source and strength, my Lord,
You are my everything, my
God, my Abba Father.

Chorus:
With every step I take,
and every breath I breathe,
both day and night,
I need You,
my Lord God.

Bridge:
You bid me come, and rest in You,
my Heavenly Father,
I look to You,
and I come Yes, I come.

Chorus:
With every step I take,
and every breath I breathe,
both day and night,
I need You,
my Lord God.

Chorus:
With every step I take,
and every breath I breathe,
both day and night,
I need You,
my Lord God.

128. Let Us Choose Eternal Life

Chorus:
Let us choose Eternal Life,
and live forever with God,
let us choose Eternal Life,
and live for-evermore
worshipping our King.

Verse:
Jesus Christ, paid the price,
to set His people free.
He bore the stripes, upon His back,
for sickness and disease.

Verse:
He wore a crown, of spike like thorns,
upon His sore pierced brow.
His hands and feet, were cruelly nailed,
on to that wooden tree.

Chorus:
Let us choose Eternal Life,
and live forever with God,
let us choose Eternal Life,
and live for-evermore
worshipping our King.

Verse:
He became sin, who knew no sin,
and died a sinners death, for you and me.
Early the third day, the
stone was rolled away,
and Jesus arose from the tomb.

Verse:
Now Jesus Christ, the Son of God,
sits on the right hand of His Father.
To know the Father, we must know the Son,
and make Him Lord of our life.

Chorus:
Let us choose Eternal Life,
and live forever with God,
let us choose Eternal Life,
and live for-evermore
worshipping our King.

Verse:
Except God's gift, of Jesus Christ,
God's only begotten Son.
Therefore, choose life, with
Lord Jesus Christ,
who died that we may live in Him.

Verse:
We are the righteousness of
God, in Christ Jesus,
redeemed from the curse of the law.
Healed and whole, made complete in Him,
walking in love, joy, peace, light and life.

Chorus:
Let us choose Eternal Life,
and live forever with God,
let us choose Eternal Life,
and live for-evermore
worshipping our King.

Verse:
Jesus's return, is at hand,
the signs are there to see.
And when He comes, to the earth again,
He'll set up His thousand year
Kingdom, and reign Victoriously.

Verse:
But if we die, before our Lords return,
we live eternally with God our Father.
The Grace of God, His unmerited favor,
has been bestowed upon us
through His Son.

Chorus:
Let us choose Eternal Life,
and live forever with God,
let us choose Eternal Life,
and live for-evermore
worshipping our King.

Verse:
God's mercy, keeps us from
what we deserve,
death, being separated from Him.
So again I say, except the
gift God has given,
and live with Him eternally.

Chorus:
Let us choose Eternal Life,
and live forever with God,
let us choose Eternal Life,
and live for-evermore
worshipping our King.

Tag:
And live forever more,
Worshipping our King.
Living for ever more worshiping our King.

Section Eight

Song Lyrics With Thankful Praise

129. Showers of Blessings

Verse:
Showers of blessings,
With rain falling down.
Softly and gently,
Soaking this thirsty ground.
I thank you my Father,
I thank you my Lord.
For showers of blessings,
From whom I adore.

Verse:
Showers of blessing,
I'm No longer dry.
God, You fill me up,
until I over flow.
I thank you my Father,
I thank you my Lord.
For showers of blessing,
From whom makes me whole.

Chorus:
You water this land, with rain from above,
With a song in my heart,
And praise on my lips,
I thank you my Father, I
thank you my Lord,
For showers of blessing, That
fill me once more.

Verse:
With showers of blessing,
And rain falling down.
So softly and gently,
You soak this thirsty ground.
I thank you my Father,
I thank you my Lord.
For showers of blessing,
From whom I adore.

Chorus:
You water this land, with rain from above,
With a song in my heart,
And praise on my lips,
I thank you my Father, I
thank you my Lord,
For showers of blessing, That
fill me once more.

Chorus:
You water this land, with rain from above,
With a song in my heart,
And praise on my lips,
I thank you my Father, I
thank you my Lord,
For showers of blessing, That
fill me once more.

130. Freely, You Gave

Verse:
Freely You gave,
gratefully I receive.
Freely You came,
joyfully I believe.

Verse:
Worthy of death,
You Jesus took my place.
Worthy of death,
You made another way.

Chorus:
Holy You are, Lord Jesus,
in all of Your ways,
Gracious and Merciful
day after day.

Verse:
Freely You paid,
as humbly I repent.
Freely forgave,
as I ask forgiveness.

Chorus:
Holy You are, Lord Jesus,
in all of Your ways,
Gracious and Merciful
day after day.

Chorus:
Holy You are, Lord Jesus,
in all of Your ways,
Gracious and Merciful
day after day.

131. It's You

Verse:
I soar above the earth as on eagles wings,
cradled in Your loving arms,
abiding in You forever more.
needing You, the Way, the
Light, and the Door.

Chorus:
It's You who brought me out of darkness.
It's You who cleansed and made me whole.
It's You who loved me even though....
It's You who gave me hope and more.
It's You, yes Lord Jesus, it is You.

Verse:
Soaring up high in the sky
free from my bonds,
fixed like as on eagles wings,
O' My Lord and God I love You so,
Ruler of all Lord, in whom I adore.

Chorus:
It's You who brought me out of darkness.
It's You who cleansed and made me whole.
It's You who loved me even though....
It's You who gave me hope and more.
It's You, yes Lord Jesus, it is You.

Verse:
I soar so very high up above the earth,
like as on eagles wings,
Your love and life has given me worth,
and has joyously set my heart to sing.

Chorus:
It's You who brought me out of darkness.
It's You who cleansed and made me whole.
It's You who loved me even though....
It's You who gave me hope and more.
It's You, yes Lord Jesus, it is You.

Chorus:
It's You who brought me out of darkness.
It's You who cleansed and made me whole.
It's You who loved me even though....
It's You who gave me hope and more.
It's You, yes Lord Jesus, it is You.

132. Only You

Verse:
My source, my strength, my life,
I look to You, I rest in You, I wait upon
You, My life, my strength, my source.

Chorus:
It's You, and only You, my God Almighty,
You are my source, You are my
strength, You are my life,
it's You and only You.

Verse:
My source, my strength, my life,
I wait upon You, I rest in You, I look to
You, my life, my strength, my source.

Chorus:
It's You, and only You, my God Almighty,
You are my source, You are my
strength, You are my life,
it's You and only You.

Verse:
My shield, my love, my rock,
I will to You, I trust in You, I lean upon
You, my rock, my love, my shield.

Chorus 2:
It's You, and only You, my God Almighty,
You are my Shield, You are my
love, You are my rock,
it's You and only You.

Verse:
My shield, my love, my rock,
I lean upon You, I trust in You, I hold
to You, my rock, my love, my shield.

Chorus 2:
It's You, and only You, my God Almighty,
You are my Shield, You are my
love, You are my rock,
it's You and only You.

Bridge:
Yes, it's You, and only You,
my God Almighty,
my source, my strength, my life,
my shield, my love, my rock,
yes, it's You and only You,
my everything, and my all in all.

Chorus:
It's You, and only You, my God Almighty,
You are my source, You are my
strength, You are my life,
it's You and only You.

Chorus 2:
It's You, and only You, my God Almighty,
You are my Shield, You are my
love, You are my rock,
it's You and only You.

Section Nine

Unlabeled Song Lyrics

133. O What Manner:

Verse:
What manner of man is this,
that he commands even
the wind and waves,
and they obey him.
O' What manner of man is this?

Verse:
What manner of man is this,
that he commands even the
devil and demons,
and they obey him.
O' What manner of man is this?

Chorus:
Jesus, came and grew
and lived out his father's love.
Jesus, spoke and prayed
and walked in his fathers will.

Verse:
What manner of man is this,
that God, took on flesh dwelling among us.
O' What manner of man is this?

Verse:
What manner of man is this,
that God, lived, died, and
rose on the third day.
O' What manner of man is this?

Bridge:
What manner,
o' what manner,
what manner of man is this?
What manner,
O' what manner,
What manner of man is this?

Chorus:
Jesus, came and grew
and lived out his father's love.
Jesus, spoke and prayed
and walked in his fathers will.

Chorus:
Jesus, came and grew
and lived out his father's love.
Jesus, spoke and prayed
and walked in his fathers will.

134. There Was A Man's Question Answered

Introduction: There was a
man who stopped
and asked this question of me.
How do you know there is a God
and where is He?
All I could do was look at him,
and then my answer came from within.

Verse:
Do you see those trees?
Do you hear those birds?
Do you feel that breeze upon your skin?
Have you seen the mountains
capped with snow?
Have you seen the valleys down below?
Have you seen the flowers grow?

Chorus:
Yes: there is a living God,
and He is everywhere we look,
open your heart and receive His love,
and ye shall not be forsook

Verse:
Did you see that bird on the wing?
Did you see the stars gleam?
Did you see the flowing stream?
How about rainbows after the rain?
How about that bear in the cane?
How 'bout nothing being the same?

Chorus:
Yes: there is a living God,
and He is everywhere we look,
open your heart and receive His love,
and ye shall not be forsook

Bridge:
God of the universe,
creator of the Earth,
and all that is within it,
give us eyes to see-
You, everywhere we look.

Chorus:
Yes: there is a living God,
and He is everywhere we look,
open your heart and receive His love,
and ye shall not be forsook

135. I Am Under Construction

Intro: Crash! boom! watch out I plea,
Here is your hardhat and visor,
from the flying debris.

Verse:
See that sign, hanging there?
What does it read?
it boldly states,
This site is under construction, walk
carefully. all along the way.

Chorus:
No stumbling or tripping, or
being felled like a tree,
like a potter with his clay, and
a sculptor chipping away,
being consumed by His fire,
purified and lifted higher.

Verse:
This is how it is
when my Father,
begins anew work
I am now under construction, walking
carefully. led by Lord God's word.

Chorus:
No stumbling or tripping, or
being felled like a tree,
like a potter with his clay, and
a sculptor chipping away,
being consumed by His fire,
purified and lifted higher.

Verse:
Trading in the hardhat
and visor,
for my helmet,
and sword of the spirit entire. with
God's shield. that will defend me.

Chorus:
No stumbling or tripping, or
being felled like a tree,
like a potter with his clay, and
a sculptor chipping away,
being consumed by His fire,
purified and lifted higher.

Verse:
Yes, I find, that I am,
in my Gods hand,
where I will stay,
I am, Under construction, finished,
not yet, but it's in the plan.

Chorus:
No stumbling or tripping, or
being felled like a tree,
like a potter with his clay, and
a sculptor chipping away,
being consumed by His fire,
purified and lifted higher.

136. God's Garden

Verse:
be fulfilled not bare.
He waters us with His holy word;
His spirit is our tie stake.
So join God's garden filled with love,
be true and real not false nor fake.

Verse:
We are God's garden,
none of us are the same in God's sight.
So let's open eyes-ears and hearts,
allowing Him to take the pain.
Let Him cultivate His plants.

Chorus:
God's beautiful plants,
are weak and fragile,
and only survive
because of His care.
That's how it is with God's love,

Bridge:
Have you seen a garden
bursting with color and life?
With roses, daisies, daffodils,
and countless more we like.
With various colors, shapes and hues,
and sweet aromas arrayed for you.
The purples, yellows, greens,
blues, pinks, oranges,
and reds displayed so true.
With all the other life
maintained within these garden walls.

Chorus:
God's beautiful plants,
are weak and fragile,
and only survive
because of His care.
That's how it is with God's love,

Chorus:
God's beautiful plants,
are weak and fragile,
and only survive
because of His care.
That's how it is with God's love,

137. Shake It Off

Verse:
all that tries to hold us back,
lay it down at Lord God's feet.
for His yoke is easy and His
burdens are light.

Verse:
all those clinging chains from the past,
try to maintain their hold,
but he who the Lord sets free is free indeed.

Chorus:
So, shake it off, shake it off,
and focus on our God.
Yes, shake it off, shake it off,
and follow God's word.
Shake it off, shake it off, shake
off all that hinders.

Verse:
All hurt than has not healed,
trust God to finish the work,
God makes whole all that is broken,
binding up the wounds.

Chorus:
So, shake it off, shake it off,
and focus on our God.
Yes, shake it off, shake it off,
and follow God's word.
Shake it off, shake it off, shake
off all that hinders.

Bridge:
Now We're walking in light,
life and love,
hope and wholeness,
VICTORIOUSLY in Christ Jesus.

Chorus:
So, shake it off, shake it off,
and focus on our God.
Yes, shake it off, shake it off,
and follow God's word.
Shake it off, shake it off, shake
off all that hinders.

Chorus:
So, shake it off, shake it off,
and focus on our God.
Yes, shake it off, shake it off,
and follow God's word.
Shake it off, shake it off, shake
off all that hinders.

138. Going Home

Verse:
From birth to death I'm on a trip,
I'm on my way back to my true home,
from wince I came, I shall return,
back with God my heavenly Father,
where my heart says I belong.

Verse:
Adopted into God's Royal Family,
has set my feet towards my true home,
there's a longing in my heart to return,
to be back with my Heavenly Father,
where my heart says I belong.

Chorus:
I'm going home someday,
back with God, my Abba Father,
God help me here until that day,
be steadfast all along the way.

Verse:
Don't weep for me when I go home,
for now I'm healed, whole, and complete,
rather rejoice, for now I am
where I longed to be,
back with my Heavenly Father,
where my heart says I belong.

Chorus:
I'm going home someday,
back with God, my Abba Father,
God help me here until that day,
be steadfast all along the way.

Bridge:
I'm setting my heart,
on Heavenly things,
along the path,
back to my true home.

Chorus:
I'm going home someday,
back with God, my Abba Father,
God help me here until that day,
be steadfast all along the way.

Chorus:
I'm going home someday,
back with God, my Abba Father,
God help me here until that day,
be steadfast all along the way.

139. The Throne of My Heart

Verse:
I choose to place the Lord,
on the throne of my heart,
right where He belongs.

Verse:
At one time the Lord, was not
on the throne of my heart,
now that's where He resides,

Chorus:
Jesus is the Lord of lords,
and the King of kings,
high and lifted up,
Lord be magnified,
for-ever and ever and ever Amen.

Bridge:
Glory hallelujah,
praise be His holy name,
glory hallelujah,
my Lord God reigns.

Chorus:
Jesus is the Lord of lords,
and the King of kings,
high and lifted up,
Lord be magnified,
for-ever and ever and ever Amen.

Chorus:
Jesus is the Lord of lords,
and the King of kings,
high and lifted up,
Lord be magnified,
for-ever and ever and ever Amen.

140. Behind the Mask

Verse:
Have you been invited to
the masquerade party,
what mask do you hide behind?
It's time to come out from behind the mask,
that hides you.

Verse:
You say, you can't, no one will
like you if they only knew,
that's not true, for God loves you,
it's not man we should be
pleasing, but God,
and Him alone.

Chorus:
The masquerade party is over,
the games have come to an end,
may the real you step forward,
and be truly fulfilled in Him.

Verse:
All your life you have been
told, you are so very ugly,
that is not true, but a lie,
a lie from the devil who hates God and,
His creation.

Chorus:
The masquerade party is over,
the games have come to an end,
may the real you step forward,
and be truly fulfilled in Him.

Bridge:
Be genuine, not false,
walk in God's truth,
and not hide behind the lies.

Chorus:
The masquerade party is over,
the games have come to an end,
may the real you step forward,
and be truly fulfilled in Him.

Chorus:
The masquerade party is over,
the games have come to an end,
may the real you step forward,
and be truly fulfilled in Him.

141. I Choose Jesus

Chorus:
I want to be by Jesus' side,
I want to walk in God's plan,
only by His commands,
I choose Jesus,
my Lord and Saviour Jesus Christ.

Verse:
I was chosen before birth,
when God called me to this earth,
He said come forth and run the race
that has been set before you.

Verse:
I was placed within my family,
then God said choose death or life,
He said choose this day peace or strife,
as for me I choose the Lord.

Chorus:
I want to be by Jesus' side,
I want to walk in God's plan,
only by His commands,
I choose Jesus,
my Lord and Saviour Jesus Christ.

Verse:
I've learned how much I am worth,
when Lord Jesus died for me,
while hanging on that old cruel tree,
Jesus said it is finished.

Chorus:
I want to be by Jesus' side,
I want to walk in God's plan,
only by His commands,
I choose Jesus,
my Lord and Saviour Jesus Christ.

Chorus:
I want to be by Jesus' side,
I want to walk in God's plan,
only by His commands,
I choose Jesus,
my Lord and Saviour Jesus Christ.

142. Its War

Chorus:
Hup two, three, four,
lift them up and set them down.
Blow the bugle, beat the drums,
wave the banners high,
and keep unified.

Verse:
The army of the Lord, is
marching off to war,
following Jesus Christ, our
commander and general.

Verse:
We are dressed in God's armor, we
are clothed in God's strength,
we go forward not turning back,
as we march into war.

Verse:
God has gone before us, the victory is ours,
in and through Jesus Christ, with
the power of His might.

Chorus:
Hup two, three, four,
lift them up and set them down.
Blow the bugle, beat the drums,
wave the banners high,
and keep unified.

Bridge:
Its war, be clothed, in God's armor,
its war, be clothed, through God's might.

Chorus:
Hup two, three, four,
lift them up and set them down.
Blow the bugle, beat the drums,
wave the banners high,
and keep unified.

Tag:
Here we go,
forward march,
hup two, three, four,
pick them up and lay them down.

Chorus:
Hup two, three, four,
lift them up and set them down.
Blow the bugle, beat the drums,
wave the banners high,
and keep unified.

143. Suddenly

Verse:
What a change, like nothing seen before,
what a God, worthy of being adored.

Verse:
What a life, made utterly brand new,
what a word, offered to me and you.

Chorus:
Suddenly here,
and suddenly there,
look to God,
and suddenly be aware,
for it is suddenly.

Verse:
What a Lord, who gave His life for us all,
what a truth, we hold on to till He calls.

Chorus:
Suddenly here,
and suddenly there,
look to God,
and suddenly be aware,
for it is suddenly.

Verse:
What a way, filled with Heavenly light,
what a hope, carried on wings in the night.

Chorus:
Suddenly here,
and suddenly there,
look to God,
and suddenly be aware,
for it is suddenly.

Tag:
Suddenly,
suddenly,
yes, suddenly,
nothing is the same,
in our God,
for it is suddenly.

Chorus:
Suddenly here,
and suddenly there,
look to God,
and suddenly be aware,
for it is suddenly.

144. Jesus Brought Me Through

Verse:
Standing at my husband's bedside,
I looked to God and called on Jesus,
I didn't fall apart for He held me together,
it was Jesus that brought me through.

Verse:
Sitting at my husband's bedside,
waiting for them to pull the plug,
I held his hand while Jesus
did not let go of me,
In cased in peace wrapped
in His loving arms.

Chorus:
It was Jesus who brought me through,
no matter what just believe,
and call on Him,
and Jesus will bring you through,
yes, Jesus will bring you through,
for what He has done for me
He'll surely do for you.

Verse:
There at my husband's bedside,
believing that God could raise him up,
if He wanted to though He
chose to take him home,
I trusted my Jesus to bring me through.

Chorus:
It was Jesus who brought me through,
no matter what just believe,
and call on Him,
and Jesus will bring you through,
yes, Jesus will bring you through,
for what He has done for me
He'll surely do for you.

Bridge:
He brought me through,
He brought me through,
couldn't have done it without Him,
Jesus brought me through.

Chorus:
It was Jesus who brought me through,
no matter what just believe,
and call on Him,
and Jesus will bring you through,
yes, Jesus will bring you through,
for what He has done for me
He'll surely do for you.

145. Jesus Rules

Verse:
One nation under God,
holding Christ's cross high,
standing united across this land,
strengthened by Almighty God's hand.

Verse:
One church in God,
lifting Christ's cross high,
with one heart firmly taking our stand,
guided by our Father God's hand.

Chorus:
From border to border,
and coast to coast,
stand up and shout aloud,
Jesus rules and our God reigns,
all across this blessed land.

Bridge:
Jesus rules,
and our God reigns,
lift Him high,
Jesus rules,
and our God reigns,
victoriously!

Chorus:
From border to border,
and coast to coast,
stand up and shout aloud,
Jesus rules and our God reigns,
all across this blessed land.

Chorus:
From border to border,
and coast to coast,
stand up and shout aloud,
Jesus rules and our God reigns,
all across this blessed land.

146. Your Truths

Verse:
You arrest me, with everything you've done.
You amaze me, with Your awesomeness.
You capture me, with freely given grace.

Verse:
You have drawn me, every step of the way.
You have called me, ever closer to Yourself.
You have shown me, something
of who You are.

Chorus:
Guide me, lead me, never let me go.
Wash me, cleanse me, making me whole.
Show me, teach me, reveal
to me Your truths.

Verse:
You're teaching me, from Your Holy Bible.
You're healing me, by Jesus Christ's stripes.
You're singing o're me, from
Heavens realms on high.

Chorus:
Guide me, lead me, never let me go.
Wash me, cleanse me, making me whole.
Show me, teach me, reveal
to me Your truths.

Bridge:
I am Your child, I seek Your face,
I look to You, for mercy, peace and grace.

Chorus:
Guide me, lead me, never let me go.
Wash me, cleanse me, making me whole.
Show me, teach me, reveal
to me Your truths.

Tag:
Never let me go,
making me whole,
reveal to me Your truths.
Yes, never let me go,
You're making me whole,
and revealing Your truths.

Chorus:
Guide me, lead me, never let me go.
Wash me, cleanse me, making me whole.
Show me, teach me, reveal
to me Your truths.

Section Ten

Song Lyrics Filled With Worship

147. Jesus' Hands

Verse:
Hands holding hands
strengthening the bonds.
Hands that heal,
anointed by God.

Verse:
Hands helping man,
pulling us from fire.
Hands reach down,
pulling us from mire.

Chorus:
Jesus' hands are
stretched out wide,
He bids us come
and be renewed in Life.

Verse:
Hands so gentle,
for all those God loves.
Hands hard to,
choosing not from above.

Chorus:
Jesus' hands are
stretched out wide,
He bids us come
and be renewed in Life.

Bridge:
He holds us
in the palm of His hand,
nothing or no one
can snatch us out,

Chorus:
Jesus' hands are
stretched out wide,
He bids us come
and be renewed in Life.

Chorus:
Jesus' hands are
stretched out wide,
He bids us come
and be renewed in Life.

148. Lord, You Are

Verse:
Lord, You, are all together lovely.
You, are all together lovely,
All together lovely, all together lovely,
Oh Lord, You, are all together
lovely, and lovely all together.

Verse:
Lord, You, are all together Holy,
You, are all together Holy,
All together Holy, all together Holy,
O Lord, You, are all together
Holy and Holy all together.

Verse:
Lord, You, are all together Mighty,
You, are all together Mighty,
All together Mighty, all together Mighty,
O Lord, You, are all together
Mighty and Mighty all together.

Verse:
Lord, You, are all together Beautiful,
You, are all together Beautiful,
All together Beautiful, all
together Beautiful,
O Lord, You, are all together Beautiful
and Beautiful all together.

Verse:
Lord, You, are all together lovely.
You, are all together lovely,
All together lovely, all together lovely,
Oh Lord, You, are all together
lovely, and lovely all together.

Verse:
Lord, You, are all together Holy,
You, are all together Holy,
All together Holy, all together Holy,
O Lord, You, are all together
Holy and Holy all together.

Verse:
Lord, You, are all together Mighty,
You, are all together Mighty,
All together Mighty, all together Mighty,
O Lord, You, are all together
Mighty and Mighty all together.

Verse:
Lord, You, are all together Beautiful,
You, are all together Beautiful,
All together Beautiful, all
together Beautiful,
O Lord, You, are all together Beautiful
and Beautiful all together.

149. One Day

Verse:
Like a spring that bubbles up
in a dry and thirsty land,
You are the water that quenches
this thirsty man.
You are the water that flows
from God's own throne,
and who ever drinks there, will
never thirst no more.

Verse:
Like a man who is starved for much
more than man can supply,
You Jesus, are the bread that
keeps this man alive.
Your precious Holy Word
fills this man inside,
You are the word of truth
and have no part of lie.

Chorus:
Jesus is God's son,
who came and took our place;
Christ is the one,
who will come again one day,
and take His church away.

Bridge:
Thank You Lord for bearing all for me,
Your precious blood was shed
and set me free.
Your precious blood was shed
and set me free,
now I am clean.

Chorus:
Jesus is God's son,
who came and took our place;
Christ is the one,
who will come again one day,
and take His church away.

Verse:
Like a spring that bubbles up
in a dry and thirsty land,
You are the water that quenches
this thirsty man.
You are the water that flows
from God's own throne,
and who ever drinks there, will
never thirst no more.

Verse:
Like a man who is starved for much
more than man can supply,
You Jesus, are the bread that
keeps this man alive.
Your precious Holy Word
fills this man inside,
You are the word of truth
and have no part of lie.

Chorus:
Jesus is God's son,
who came and took our place;
Christ is the one,
who will come again one day,
and take His church away.

150. I Am Nothing Without You

Verse:
I am nothing without you,
a piece of dirt from which I grew,
Loving hands have molded me,
like a potter with his clay.

Chorus:
I am nothing, nothing without You,
I can do nothing, nothing without You,
For You are my everything, You are my
all in all, In You I have my being.

Verse:
Sons of God, Joint Heirs with Christ,
Kings and Priests, who have won the fight,
God's mighty army, whose battle is won,
with Jesus at its head.

Chorus:
I am nothing, nothing without You,
I can do nothing, nothing without You,
For You are my everything, You are my
all in all, In You I have my being.

Verse:
When the sun shall cease to shine,
and the moon turns to blood,
Jesus comes back in the clouds,
and takes us all away.

Chorus:
I am nothing, nothing without You,
I can do nothing, nothing without You,
For You are my everything, You are my
all in all, In You I have my being.

Verse:
We are nothing without you,
A piece of dirt from which we grew,
Loving hands have molded us,
like a potter with his clay

Chorus:
I am nothing, nothing without You,
I can do nothing, nothing without You,
For You are my everything, You are my
all in all, In You I have my being.

151. I Choose You

Chorus:
I choose You, who first chose me,
My Abba Father, my Creator,
My God Almighty,
Thank You for choosing me.

Verse:
I choose you, who is my all,
I choose you, who is my strength,
I choose you, who gave me life,
I choose you, Lord-God, I choose you.

Chorus:
I choose You, who first chose me,
My Abba Father, my Creator,
My God Almighty,
Thank You for choosing me.

Verse:
I choose you, who broke my bonds,
I choose you, who bore my stripes,
I choose you, who healed my wounds,
I choose you, Lord-God, I choose you.

Chorus:
I choose You, who first chose me,
My Abba Father, my Creator,
My God Almighty,
Thank You for choosing me.

Verse:
I choose you, who is my hope,
I choose you, who is my joy,
I choose you, who died for me,
I choose you, Lord-God, I choose you.

Verse:
I choose you, who is my Lord,
I choose you, who is my God,
I choose you, who's coming back,
I choose you, Lord-God,
Who first chose me,
I now choose You.

Chorus:
I choose You, who first chose me,
My Abba Father, my Creator,
My God Almighty,
Thank You for choosing me.

152. I Come To You

Verse:
I come to You, with my
hands held out, empty,
but You load me up with daily benefits.
I come to You, in all my weakness,
but You give me all the strength I need.
I come to You, in all my insecurities
that's when, in You I am made truly secure.

Verse:
I come to You, fresh from a battle,
but You bid me lay and rest in You.
I come to You, with a broken heart bruised,
but You heal each and every
one of my wounds.
I come to You, doubting it will work,
that's when, Lord, Your grace is sufficient.

Chorus:
I come to You, I come to You,
I come to You my Lord Jesus.
I come to You, I come to You,
I come to You Almighty God.

Verse:
I come to You, with a cloak of heaviness,
but You exchange it for a garment of praise,
I come to You, burdened down with fear,
but from You is no spirit of fear,
I come to You, thinking alone,
that's when, You're with me and never leave.

Chorus:
I come to You, I come to You,
I come to You my Lord Jesus.
I come to You, I come to You,
I come to You Almighty God.

Bridge:
I thank You, my awesome God,
and rejoice in Your Holy name,
for You are worthy of all,
glory, honor, and praise.
I magnify You, and worship You,
who are, forever the same.
my life is in You, and I need You,
in whom is my everything.

Chorus:
I come to You, I come to You,
I come to You my Lord Jesus.
I come to You, I come to You,
I come to You Almighty God.

153. My Heavenly Daddy

Pre Chorus:
Abba Father, Heavenly Daddy,
with none can be compared.

Chorus:
You are my Abba Father,
you are my Heavenly Daddy,
You are my Abba Father,
of whom I truly adore.

Verse:
You called me out of darkness,
into Your marvelous light,
You've taken me out of death,
into eternal life.

Verse:
Born in the womb of Your love,
held in Your cradling arms,
You breathed life into me,
and awoke a flame of love.

Pre Chorus:
Abba Father, Heavenly Daddy,
With none can be compared.

Chorus:
You are my Abba Father,
you are my Heavenly Daddy,
You are my Abba Father,
of whom I truly adore.

Bridge:
I love You,
my Abba Father,
I love You,
my Heavenly Daddy,
I love You,
who loves me even more.

Pre Chorus:
Abba Father, Heavenly Daddy,
with none can be compared.

Chorus:
You are my Abba Father,
you are my Heavenly Daddy,
You are my Abba Father,
of whom I truly adore.

154. I Acknowledge You

Verse:
My God and my Lord,
I acknowledge You,
my Heavenly King,
my all in all.

Verse:
The Light of my life,
my source and my strength,
my Almighty God,
my everything.

Chorus:
You are, worthy to be praised,
I acknowledge You as God,
and as Lord Supreme,
You are King of everything,
and are, greatly to be praised.

Verse:
The one and only,
my true living God,
my awesome defender,
ruling justly.

Verse:
There is none like You,
author of our faith,
the first and the Last,
the Prince of Peace.

Chorus:
You are, worthy to be praised,
I acknowledge You as God,
and as Lord Supreme,
You are King of everything,
and are, greatly to be praised.

Bridge:
Holy, and Righteous,
Pure, and Just,
Faithful, and True,
Merciful, and Gracious,
Kind, and Good.

Chorus:
You are, worthy to be praised,
I acknowledge You as God,
and as Lord Supreme,
You are King of everything,
and are, greatly to be praised.

155. We Worship You

Chorus:
We give You glory,
we give You honor,
we give You praise,
we adore you,
we worship You Almighty God.

Verse:
Revere God and give Him all
glory, honor and praise in worship,
for the hour of His judgments has arrived,
Fall down before Him,
pay Him homage and adoration,
and worship Him who created
Heaven and earth.

Chorus:
We give You glory,
we give You honor,
we give You praise,
we adore you,
we worship You Almighty God.

Bridge:
Proclaim the Good News,
to every tribe and race
and language and people.

Chorus:
We give You glory,
we give You honor,
we give You praise,
we adore you,
we worship You Almighty God.

Verse:
Revere God and give Him all
glory, honor and praise in worship,
for the hour of His judgments has arrived,
Fall down before Him,
pay Him homage and adoration,
and worship Him who created
Heaven and earth,
yes, worship Him who created
heaven and earth.

Chorus:
We give You glory,
we give You honor,
we give You praise,
we adore you,
we worship You Almighty God.

156. More of You

Verse:
Jesus lover of my soul,
I'm seeking for You,
I want more of You Lord,
much more of You,
more than ever before.

Verse:
Jesus Saviour of my life,
I'm thirsting for You,
I thirst for more of You Lord,
much more of You,
more of You than ever before.

Chorus:
More of You, much more of You,
I'm running to You Lord,
more of You, much more of You,
I want more of You Jesus.

Verse:
Jesus light of my world,
I'm hungering for You,
I hunger for more of You Lord,
much more of You,
more than ever before.

Chorus:
More of You, much more of You,
I'm running to You Lord,
more of You, much more of You,
I want more of You Jesus.

Bridge:
O Lord Jesus,
I'm seeking for You,
thirsting for You,
hungering for You,
more than ever before.

Chorus:
More of You, much more of You,
I'm running to You Lord,
more of You, much more of You,
I want more of You Jesus.

Tag:
More of You, much more of You,
more of You, much more of You Lord,
more of You, much more of You,
more of You, much more of You Jesus.

157. Jesus Is Enough

Chorus:
Jesus is enough,
and has done the work,
God is love,
and gave us choice.

Verse:
Jesus, Yes, You are enough,
Yes, Jesus, You are the truth,
the life, and the way,
my Everything, and my all in all,
and the Saviour of my soul.

Verse:
Father, Yes, Your word is life,
Yes, Father, Your will and ways
are higher than mine,
my Creator and Ancient of days,
and my God Almighty.

Chorus:
Jesus is enough,
and has done the work,
God is love,
and gave us choice.

Bridge:
You gave us the Choice to choose,
Blessing or cursing,
Life or death,
Light or dark,
Right or wrong,
so choose Jesus,
and make Him Lord.

Chorus:
Jesus is enough,
and has done the work,
God is love,
and gave us choice.

Chorus:
Jesus is enough,
and has done the work,
God is love,
and gave us choice.

Printed in the United States
By Bookmasters